I0192171

# Sunday School Lessons

## from the

## Gospel

## according to

## John

# Mark

## Commentaries and Lessons

## by

# Larry D. Alexander

**REVISED SECOND EDITION**

Copyright © 2006 - 2016 by Larry D. Alexander

All rights reserved. Printed the in U.S.A.

ISBN # 978-0-6151-3552-6

No part of this book may be reproduced
for any purpose except for brief excerpts
regarding  reviews or articles by magazines,
newspapers or broadcast, and, use in churches
for Sunday school, bible study, etc.
without the express written consent of the publisher.

Larry D. Alexander
214-649-7671

Cover designed by
Larry D. Alexander

**OTHER BOOKS ON CHRISTIANITY BY LARRY D. ALEXANDER INCLUDE:**

*\* Sunday school lessons from the book of the Acts of the Apostles*
*\* Sunday school lessons from the Apostle Paul's letter to the Romans*
*\* Home Bible study commentaries from the Gospel of John*
*\* Home and Church Bible study commentaries from the book of Hebrews*
*\* Home and Church Bible study commentaries from Paul's letter to the Romans*
*\*Home and Church Bible Study Commentaries from Galatians, Ephesians, & Philippians*

# I

## INTRODUCTION

Larry D. Alexander is a well-known visual artist, turned Christian teacher and author, who was called by GOD, more than eleven years ago, to learn and teach HIS Holy Word, without help from the institutions of men. He understood his calling to be that his training in the Word was to be infused in him, through direct guidance from GOD, through the HOLY SPIRIT, and that GOD will always lead him spiritually to the right material, people, and sources that he needs, in order to successfully do HIS Will. Alexander says GOD instructed him to began to write down, and retain in writing, those things that he had learned, and then, to share them with others. Alexander has been teaching Sunday school and bible studies for the past ten years.

This book is written to help revive the interest of adults in building themselves up in the Word of GOD by attending Home and Church Bible studies and Sunday school classes in their respective Christian churches, and, to start up, or restore Bible studies and Sunday school classes back to those Christian churches that are lacking these opportunities to get to know CHRIST JESUS, our LORD. Alexander strongly believes that the only thing that can change a man or woman for the better is the Word of GOD.

All of Alexander's books are designed to promote spiritual growth and right-living in those who choose to read and incorporate GOD's directives into their everyday lives. The teaching commentaries that are presented in this book, as well as Alexander's previous books are bold and straightforward. They are to be used to help introduce people to JESUS through a study of the words and actions that were demonstrated to us by JESUS, during HIS three-year ministry here on earth, and, through the work of the Apostles and others who were instrumental in the development and establishment of the early Christian Church. Again there is a strong focus on developing good Christian living practices and behavior, and, on developing a fear and reverence for the ONLY WISE GOD, WHO is our SAVIOR, through JESUS CHRIST, HIS SON, WHO sent to us, the HOLY SPIRIT.

# INTRODUCTION TO THE BOOK OF MARK

The, gospel account of Mark, along with Matthew's and Luke's gospel accounts, are known collectively, as the "Synoptic Gospels". The word "synoptic" comes from a combination of two Greek words, which mean, "to see together". These three gospel accounts can be set down, side by side, and their common contents, can and should, perhaps, be viewed and examined together.

The book of Mark is widely believed by scholars, to be the earliest of the four gospel accounts, even though it is situated second to Matthew in the bible assemblage. It is also the shortest and most straightforward of the four gospels.

Many scholars believe, that, because John Mark's blunt use of the Greek language reflects that of the common man, and also, because of his use of Latin constructions, or expressions, in his transliterations, his gospel account was aimed at convincing the Roman populace of the divinity of CHRIST JESUS.

John Mark's account of JESUS' life is almost certainly, according to strong evidence from Jewish tradition, a writing down of the Apostle Peter's account of his life experiences being an integral part of JESUS' three-year earthbound ministry. Most scholars also believe that John Mark was not, himself, an eyewitness to most of the scenes that he so vividly depicts in his gospel account. However, the great Church historian Eusebius, quotes a document written by Papias circa A.D. 140, that cites the Apostle John as verifying Mark's gospel account as being dictated by the Apostle Peter.

Mark's gospel picks up JESUS' story, just prior to HIS baptism by John the Baptist in the river Jordan, and leads us through to Golgotha, and beyond, to the climax at Judea. Scripture also paints a fascinating picture of John Mark, as we see him mentioned several times throughout the book of Acts (Acts 12:12, 12:25, 13:5, 13:13 & 15:36-41) and, in Colossians 4:10, Philemon 24, 2 Timothy 4:11, and 1 Peter 5:13.

John Mark was the cousin of Barnabas, and traveled with, he and Paul, on their first missionary journey together (Acts 13:4-14). However, John Mark abandoned Paul and Barnabas and left them, while at Pamphylia, and because of Mark's actions there, Barnabas and Paul split up just prior to their second missionary journey. Paul then chose Silas to travel with him, and Barnabas, went on to travel with Mark.

It turned out, however, that, Barnabas did the right thing by not giving up on young John Mark as he went on to develop into a very effective missionary, later making up with Paul, and also, becoming the author of one of the most important books ever written.

# CONTENTS

*INTRODUCTION*------------------------------------------------- *I*

*INTRODUCTION TO THE BOOK OF MARK*-------------------- *II*

JESUS BEGINS HIS MINISTRY------------------------------------- 1

THE BEGINNING OF CONFLICT-------------------------------- 5

MIRACLE HEALINGS------------------------------------------------ 9

THE TRUE FAMILY OF JESUS-------------------------------------- 12

CALMING THE STORM------------------------------------------- 15

THE SIGNIFICANCE OF HAVING FAITH--------------------- 19

REJECTION AND MISSION------------------------------------- 23

A LITTLE IS A LOT IN THE HANDS OF JESUS--------------- 26

WHAT REALLY DEFILES-------------------------------------- 29

JESUS: A GOOD THAT IS ALSO LOVELY-------------------- 33

AFFIRMATION AND CONFESSION OF FAITH-------------- 37

HONEST FAITH---------------------------------------------------- 41

THE INSTITUTION OF MARRIAGE---------------------------- 44

THE DANGERS OF PROSPERITY------------------------------ 48

FAITH AND SIGHT------------------------------------------------- 51

JESUS' TRIUMPHANT ENTRY INTO JERUSALEM-------- 56

THE MOST IMPORTANT COMMANDMENT------------------ 60

A NEW MEANING FOR PASSOVER---------------------------- 63

# CONTENTS

JESUS ON TRIAL------------------------------------------------- 70

JESUS' CRUCIFIXION--------------------------------------------- 76

THE RESURRECTION OF CHRIST--------------------------- 81

CLOSING PRAYER------------------------------------------------- 85

**LESSON ONE:**

# JESUS BEGINS HIS MINISTRY
## (The proof of JESUS' authority was shown through HIS actions)

## SCRIPTURE:
### The King James Version
### (Mark 1:9-28)

**1** (9) And it came to pass in those days, that JESUS came from Nazareth of Galilee, and was baptized of John in Jordan. (10) And straightway coming up out of the water, he saw the heavens opened, and the SPIRIT like a dove descending upon HIM: (11) And there came a VOICE from heaven, saying, "THOU art my beloved SON, in WHOM I am well pleased". (12) And immediately the SPIRIT driveth HIM into the wilderness. (13) And HE was there in the wilderness forty days, tempted of satan; and was with the wild beasts; and the angels ministered unto HIM. (14) Now after that John was put in prison, JESUS came into Galilee, preaching the gospel of the kingdom of GOD, (15) And saying, "The time is fulfilled, and the kingdom of GOD is at hand: repent ye, and believe the gospel". (16) Now as HE walked by the sea of Galilee, HE saw Simon and Andrew his brother casting a net into the sea: for they were fishers. (17) And JESUS said unto them, "Come ye after ME, and I will make you to become fishers of men". (18) And straightway they forsook their nets, and followed HIM. (19) And when HE had gone a little farther thence, HE saw James the son of Zebedee, and John his brother, who also were in the ship mending their nets. (20) And straightway HE called them: and they left their father Zebedee in the ship with the hired servants, and went after HIM. (21) And they went into Capernaum; and straightway on the sabbath day HE entered into the synagogue, and taught. (22) And they were astonished at HIS doctrine: for HE taught them as one that had authority, and not as the scribes. (23) And there was in their synagogue a man with an unclean spirit; and he cried out, (24) saying, "Let us alone; what have we to do with THEE, THOU JESUS of Nazareth? art THOU come to destroy us? I know THEE WHO THOU art, the HOLY ONE of GOD. (25) And JESUS rebuked HIM, saying, "Hold thy peace, and come out of him". (26) And when the unclean spirit had torn him, and cried with a loud voice, he came out of him. (27) And they were all amazed, insomuch that they questioned among themselves, saying, "What thing is this? What new doctrine is this? For with authority commandeth HE even the unclean spirits, and they do obey HIM. (28) And immediately HIS fame spread abroad throughout all the region round about Galilee.

## COMMENTARY:

In the Gospel according to Mark, as expressed in the original Greek, the word John Mark uses for "straightway" is "euthus"(yoo-thoos), and it is used more than forty times in his Gospel account. It describes the "urgency" by which JESUS tackled his ministry from the moment HE stepped out of the River Jordan, after being baptized by HIS cousin and forerunner, John the Baptist.

Mark records that JESUS was then, immediately compelled into the wilderness by the HOLY SPIRIT, where he faced the temptations of Satan after forty days of fasting. Scripture also tells us that HE dwelt with the wild beasts, and after this trying ordeal, HE was then ministered to by angels from heaven.

Right away, the first thing this passage teaches us is that, in this life in the human flesh, here on earth, even JESUS could not escape the assault of temptation from satan. It should also be understood that temptations, or urges to do evil, do not from GOD, but rather, they come from satan. Those temptations are meant to make us fail under GOD, and lead us farther and farther away from HIM.

We ourselves need to know that GOD cannot be tempted, and just as GOD cannot be tempted to do evil, HE also will not tempt any of his human creation to do evil (James 1:13). However, GOD does put us through certain tests of struggles and difficulties in life, in an attempt to make us stronger so that we can withstand the wiles of the devil. These tests actually show us, at any given moment, just how far we are from, or how close we are to leaving GOD's Will for us in life. They are tests from which, hopefully, we will be strengthened, and thereby, emerge as better warriors for CHRIST.

And so we see here in this gospel account of Mark, that, even JESUS had to first show the strength of HIS faith, before HE could demand that we show ours. This gospel account also seeks to show us that GOD is interested in what we do, not what we say. It is meant to focus our attention on JESUS' actions, more so, than on HIS words. JESUS, sought to teach mankind how to serve GOD through our behavior, and, through our actions.

"Follow ME, and I will make you fishers of men" is what JESUS said, first, to Peter and Andrew. But it is also an invitation that comes to us, from across the spans of time, in hopes that we too, will accept HIS holy summons. Into every life, there comes many moments in which we must decide which things we're going to accept, and which things we need to reject. JESUS accepted the final phase of HIS earthly mission from HIS FATHER GOD that day, on the banks of the River Jordan, and the world will never be the same as it was before HE did.

The undecided life is the most wasted life there is, and here in Mark 1:9-11, JESUS recognized, when HIS moment of decision had come. No doubt HIS earthly home in Nazareth may have been peaceful and comfortable, however, GOD does not call HIS people to peace and comfort on earth because HE doesn't want to tempt us to fall in love with this world.

JESUS had already given up a greater peace and comfort in Heaven than here on earth, and even though the peace of GOD also abided with HIM in HIS earthly home, it was time to give it all up and complete HIS commission from the FATHER. For us it becomes a question of, "How bad do we want Salvation?" Do we want it bad enough to relinquish the people and things of this world? We as Christians must desire to accept the gift of salvation just as much as JESUS desired to give it to us.

A good example of the wrong attitude, and its effect on our decision-making, comes in the story of the rich young ruler, which we will see later in Mark 10. There we'll see that, just moments after the rich young man had shut himself off from Heaven, by refusing to give up his riches to follow JESUS, that, our LORD and SAVIOR responded to a comment made by Peter, regarding his observation of the incident that had just transpired with the young aristocrat. There JESUS states, "Verily I say unto you, there is no man that hath left house, or brethren, or sisters, or father, or mother, or wife, or children, or lands, for MY sake, and the gospel's, but he shall receive an hundredfold now in this time, houses, and brethren, and sisters, and mothers, and children, and lands, with persecutions; and in the world to come eternal life. But many that are first shall be last; and the last first" (KJV).

A person may have to sacrifice many ties that are near and dear to them, in order to become a follower of CHRIST. But when they do, they become members of an eternal family and brotherhood that is as wide as the Heaven and the Earth. JESUS tells us "straightway" that to be a Christian is a costly thing, and certainly we will receive our rewards. But we must first prove ourselves to be big enough, to have and to hold our position. And that is what JESUS' vicarious sacrifice did, and does, for all us, and that is also, what HIS wonderful mission from GOD, was all about.


## PERSONAL APPLICATION:

(1). Can a person look at you on any given day and be able to see, from your actions, that JESUS is the head of your life?

(2). If you are already a professed Christian, in what areas of your life do you find it most difficult to submit to CHRIST, wholeheartedly?

(3). After you profess to Christianity, there is going to be many times, as you study the Word of GOD, when GOD's instructions will go against your human desires, however, you must continue to strengthen yourself, through His word, and, through persistent prayer, so that you will be able to overcome these weaknesses.

(4). Remember, whenever anyone comes to CHRIST to receive salvation, satan is going to increase his efforts, to try to get them to stumble and fall back, before they can fully accept CHRIST in their heart. So Beware, and be strong.

## LIFE RESPONSE:

Pray to GOD right now, that HE will give you strength to eliminate, one sin at a time, from your life that you may have tried to hang on to, even though you knew they were wrong. And ask for HIS forgiveness, through earnest repentance of your heart.

## KEY VERSE:

"Come ye after ME, and I will make you to become fishers of men"- Mark 1:17

DEVOTIONAL PASSAGES: Matthew 4:19, John 21:15, John 20:21

# LESSON TWO:

(5)

## THE BEGINNING OF CONFLICT
(The miracle of GOD's forgiveness is needed to relieve the burden of sin)

### SCRIPTURE:
The King James Version
(Mark 2:1-17)

**2** (1) And again HE entered into Capernaum after some days; and it was noised that HE was in the house. (2) And straightway many were gathered together, insomuch that there was no room to receive them, no, not so much as about the door: and HE preached the word unto them. (3) And they come unto HIM, bringing one sick of the palsy, which was born of four. (4) And when they could not come nigh unto HIM for the press, they uncovered the roof where HE was: and when they had broken it up, they let down the bed wherein the sick of the palsy lay. (5) When JESUS saw their faith, HE said unto the sick of the palsy, "Son, thy sins be forgiven thee". (6) But there were certain of the scribes sitting there, and reasoning in their hearts, (7) "Why doth this MAN thus speak blasphemies? Who can forgive sins but GOD only?" (8) And immediately when JESUS perceived in HIS SPIRIT that they so reasoned within themselves, HE said unto them, "Why reason ye these things in your hearts? (9) Whether is it easier to say to the sick of the palsy, thy sins be forgiven thee; or to say, arise, and take up thy bed, and walk? (10) But that ye may know that the SON OF MAN hath power on earth to forgive sins, (HE saith to the sick of the palsy,) (11) I say unto thee, arise, and take up thy bed, and go thy way into thine house." (12) And immediately he arose, took up the bed, and went forth before them all; insomuch that they were all amazed, and glorified GOD, saying, "We never saw it on this fashion." (13) And HE went forth again by the sea side; and all the multitude resorted unto HIM, and HE taught them. (14) And as HE passed by, HE saw Levi the son of Alphaeus sitting at the receipt of custom, and said unto him, "Follow ME". And he arose and followed HIM. (15) And it came to pass, that, as JESUS sat at meat in his house, many publicans and sinners sat also together with JESUS and HIS disciples: for there were many, and they followed HIM. (16) And when the scribes and Pharisees saw HIM eat with publicans and sinners, they said unto HIS disciples, "How is it that HE eateth and drinketh with publicans and sinners? (17) When JESUS heard it, HE saith unto them, "They that are whole have no need of the physician but they that are sick: I came not to call the righteous, but the sinners to repentance."

(6)

## COMMENTARY:

In Mark chapter two, verse five, the word John Mark uses for "forgiven", in the original Greek, is "aphiemi"(ap-i-mee), and it means, quite literally, "to send away" or "wipe away", in this case, "sin". Those who argue that JESUS never claimed to be GOD, simply choose to ignore this passage (Mark 2:5-12). But true Christians already know that only GOD can "send away" or "wipe away" our sins.

JESUS clearly makes that claim that day, from a little house in Capernaum where HE first, healed the paralyzed man spiritually by forgiving his sins, and then, proved HIS claim by healing him physically. This story serves as a reminder that the first thing JESUS does for each of us is to say "thy sins be forgiven thee".

The true essence of JESUS' life is that, through HIM, we see clearly depicted, GOD's attitude towards mankind, HIS greatest creation. It is not an attitude of wanting to always apply stern justice or continuous demands on our person, but rather, it is an attitude of discipline through "perfect love", and having a heart that yearns eagerly to forgive us. And while GOD won't change HIS rules of life for us, HE will always, through tests and time, try to gradually move us back into HIS Will where we can inherit eternal life.

In Mark 2:13-14, we see JESUS' call for Matthew, a hated Tax Collector, to "follow ME". This, of course, was much to the displeasure of both the other Disciples, and to the Pharisees. Being a Tax Collector, Matthew was one of the most hated men in town. But fortunately, JESUS always wants the man that no one else wants.

Of all the Disciples, Matthew probably gave up the most to follow JESUS. When he left his Tax Collector job that day, he automatically burned his bridges with the Romans. There could be no return to such a position of trust in the Roman government by a Jewish citizen. He had made a decision on faith that would cut him off from all that he had known in his adult life. But again, the person who has contempt or fear in his heart can never be a "fisherman of men" anyway.

It was Charles .T. Studs, the great 20th century missionary for Christ, who had an outstanding quote that he always loved to use. He would often say that, "Some people want to live within the sound of the Church, or Chapel bell, I want to run a rescue shop for souls, within a yard of Hell".

The miracle of JESUS' forgiveness transformed Matthew from being one of the most hated men in town, into becoming the author of, perhaps, the most important book, the world will ever read. When Matthew left his Tax Collector's table that day, he gave up much in the material sense, however, in the spiritual sense he became heir to a fortune.

We too must one day step up and invest our treasures in the Kingdom of Heaven, and it would be best if we stake our claim right now. In fact, each day that we fail to do so, really could be, our very last chance. JESUS is saying to us now, what HE said to Matthew then, and since we don't know when our last opportunity may come, let us stake our claim right now on that which are in Heaven, on a place that, JESUS says, has already been prepared for us, since the foundation of this World.

## PERSONAL APPLICATION:

(1). There are three categories of sin burdens that human beings suffer and struggle with; the first is the burden of past sin that we fear will come back to haunt us. Even after we become Christian, some of us don't quite grasp the power of GOD's forgiveness, on our lives. The death of our LORD and SAVIOR, JESUS CHRIST, on the cross, allows us to obtain full forgiveness from GOD, for our past sins.

(2). Then there are those who have a present, or current struggle with a sin that they cannot seem to overcome. Perhaps it could be an uncontrollable anger, or some other stronghold that we're having a problem overcoming, and even though we pray after each incident for GOD's forgiveness, we really don't feel GOD will forgive us, because we keep doing it over and over again. JESUS' vicarious sacrifice covers all of our present sins.

(3). And finally, there are those who suffer with a cause-and-effect burden regarding their sin. In other words, they feel that they are the cause, through their sin, for any past hurts in their lives, and they feel GOD will let them continue to suffer for the rest of their lives. And so, they are afraid to move on into the future for fear that they will make another unforgivable mistake. They, like the previous two examples, do not trust in GOD's forgiveness. JESUS' sacrifice on the cross covers all future sins.

(4). Our burden should not be a fear that GOD will not keep HIS promise of forgiveness, for the GOD of creation cannot lie. Our responsibility lies in our willingness to "earnestly repent" for our sins, so that we may obtain GOD's gracious forgiveness. The word "repent" means "a change of mind", but it is a change of mind "before you sin". We have to learn to change our minds while still in the "thinking stages" of sin. We have to understand that true repent is a thing of the heart, not just words, or even actions. GOD determines our sincerity by reading our hearts, not our lips.

**LIFE RESPONSE:**

Pray earnestly for GOD's forgiveness of your trespasses against HIM, and also pray for strength and courage to go forward in the mighty name of JESUS, in an earnest effort to sin no more. Pray that HE help you to stay focused on the life-example of CHRIST, so that you may always be able to reflect HIS image to others, through your own behavior.

**KEY VERSE: Mark 2:17**

**DEVOTIONAL PASSAGES: Matthew 5:27-30, Luke 15:1-7, 1 John 1:9 & Ephesians 1:7**

# LESSON THREE:

## MIRACLE HEALINGS
### (Don't let your stubbornness limit GOD's blessing)

## SCRIPTURE:
### The King James Version
### (Mark 3:1-6)

**3** **(1)** And HE entered again into the synagogue; and there was a man there which had a withered hand. **(2)** And they watched HIM, whether HE would heal him on the Sabbath day; that they might accuse HIM. **(3)** And HE saith unto the man which had the withered hand, "Stand forth". **(4)** And HE saith unto them, "Is it lawful to do good on the Sabbath days, or to do evil? To save life, or to kill?" but they held their peace. **(5)** And when HE had looked round about on them with anger, being grieved for the hardness of their hearts, HE saith unto the man, "Stretch forth thine hand". And he stretched it out: and his hand was restored whole as the other. **(6)** And the Pharisees went forth, and straightway took counsel with the Herodians against HIM, how they might destroy HIM.

## COMMENTARY:

Flavius Josephus, the great Jewish historian and general in the Galilean Army writes in chapter 7 of his now historic work, "The wars of the Jews", that, when the great Roman general Pompey was besieging Jerusalem in 63 B.C., the Jews took refuge inside the walls of the temple precincts.

Pompey proceeded to build a huge dirt-ramp mound up against the wall from which he would attempt to attack and overtake the temple. He knew, that, because of the Jews religious beliefs regarding "doing no kind of work on the Sabbath", not even to defend themselves in war, it would allow him to easily build this mound without resistance from the Jewish soldiers if he worked on the mound only on the Sabbath.

And so he ordered his men to construct this mound, working only on the Sabbath days, and true to form, no Jew lifted a finger to stop them, even though they knew, by doing so, that they were signing their own death warrants. Pompey was then able to go on and capture the city of Jerusalem and the rest is history. This incident shows us how serious the Jews took their honoring of the Sabbath day law.

In Mark chapter 3, verses 1-6, John Mark gives us a vivid description of a case scenario where the tradition of "the Sabbath day honor" is still alive and well in Israel nearly 100 years later. Here he tells us that on the Sabbath Day JESUS, once again enters into the temple to teach.

On this occasion JESUS encounters a man who is afflicted with a shriveled hand. The original Greek writing hints that this man was probably not born that way, as it translates that his hand was "made normal again". JESUS knew full well that the man's life wasn't in the least bit of danger and HE could have very easily waited until the following day to heal him. JESUS simply viewed this as a "test case" of sorts, that, HE might use to override the ancient, misguided perception of what GOD's true intent was, for the purpose of the Sabbath day law.

JESUS knew that the religious leaders were watching and waiting to see if HE would attempt a healing on the Sabbath, that actually, bore no urgency. Saddened, by the hard-heartedness of these leaders in particular, JESUS commands that the man come forth, and, stretch out his hand so everyone there could see his deformity.

Then JESUS posed a rhetorical, four-part question to the misguided temple audience. Here HE asks, "Is it lawful to do "good" on the Sabbath? Or, is it lawful to do evil on the Sabbath? Should a man be able to save a life on the Sabbath, if he can, or, should he allow someone to die, just because it is the Sabbath?"

Faced with these thought-provoking inquiries, the Pharisees remained silent. And the silence moved JESUS to anger, because, when faced with choosing the method of action most consistent with the purpose of the Sabbath day law, the religious leaders of the day, failed even to respond. When the man stretched out his hand in faith, his hand was completely restored.

One can't help but notice in the text, that JESUS never even touched the man's hand at all. There was nothing visible to suggest that JESUS did anything physical that could be viewed as "work on the Sabbath", during this miracle healing. Here, JESUS clearly demonstrates that HE is LORD of even the Sabbath. In HIS not touching the man, JESUS quite literally releases this act of healing from the legal encumbrances of the law, and, at one and the same time, in HIS wonderful grace, HE delivers the man from his distressful condition.

One would think that this course of action, by JESUS, would satisfy all concerned parties in the temple that day. But instead, we see in this scene (verse 6), what turned out to be the climax of JESUS' conflict with the religious community in Galilee. And we see also, that this becomes, in this book of Mark, John Mark's first explicit reference to JESUS' death.

Despite the miraculous healing that day in the temple at Capernaum, on the northern shore of the Sea of Galilee, the Pharisees persisted in their stubbornness to not accept JESUS as the long-awaited MESSIAH. They could only conclude, in their shallow minds, that, anyone who would break the Sabbath Law, could only be a sinner, and certainly could not be, the SON of the LIVING GOD.

And, although the masses were rapidly beginning to recognize JESUS as the, much anticipated Messiah, the knowledgeable Pharisees were growing ever cool to such a thought, and in fact, joined forces with their prior enemies, the Herodians, and sought to bring JESUS life, and mission to an end.

## PERSONAL APPLICATION:

(1). More than anything else this story points out the depth of the Pharisees pride. Have you been letting your pride block you from the blessings of GOD?

(2). Acting out of envy the Pharisees collaborated with their enemies to remove JESUS from their lives permanently. Do you continue to let envy block you from the blessings GOD?

(3). The positive figure in this story, other than JESUS, is the man of faith, with the inadequate hand. Next to CHRIST, all of our hands look withered, and that is why we need HIM to make us whole and more useful. GOD sent us CHRIST JESUS, to redeem, and, to restore us, to a right relationship with HIM. But we must be willing to resist pride and envy, and bring ourselves low to receive the honor that humility can bring.

## LIFE RESPONSE:

Pray to GOD and thank HIM for HIS grace and toleration of the foolish pride and envy, which has stubbornly found a stronghold in your life. Pray that HE helps you to leave behind, all the stubbornness that is keeping you from realizing the fullness of HIS blessings. And then, ask that HE humbles your heart and issues you the strength to remain humble in your heart, all the days of your life.

KEY VERSE: Mark 3:5

DEVOTIONAL PASSAGES: John 9:1-12, Mark 5:25-34, & Mark 9:17-29

## THE TRUE FAMILY OF JESUS
### (The true conditions of kinship with CHRIST)

### SCRIPTURE:
The King James Version
(Mark 3:21 & 31-35)

**3** (20) And the multitude cometh together again, so that they could not so much as eat bread. (21) And when HIS friends heard of it, they went out to lay hold on HIM: for they said, "HE is beside HIMSELF". (31) There came then HIS brethren and HIS mother, and, standing without, sent unto HIM, calling HIM. (32) And the multitude sat about HIM, and they said unto HIM, "Behold, thy mother and thy brethren without seek for THEE". (33) And HE answered them, saying, "Who is MY mother, or MY brethren?" (34) And HE looked round about on them which sat about HIM, and said, "Behold MY mother and MY brethren! (35) For whosoever shall do the will of GOD, the same is MY brother, and MY sister, and mother".

### COMMENTARY:

"HE was in the world, and the world was made by HIM, and the world knew HIM not. HE came unto HIS own, and HIS own received HIM not. But as many as received HIM, to them gave HE power to become the sons of GOD, even to them that believe on HIS name" (John 1:10-12).

This is perhaps the key passage in scripture that lets us know, that, we can be human and not necessarily be a child of GOD. And for those of you who think, your being born into the human race, automatically qualifies you, this verse tells us we need to think again.

Here, in these statements, the apostle John clearly tells us that we, as human beings are not automatically "a child of GOD". In this passage, he states that the criteria for such a privilege, requires us to first accept and believe on the name of JESUS CHRIST.

In Mark chapter 3, verses 20-21, we find JESUS and HIS original disciples in a little house in Capernaum, being pressed by a great crowd of people. In fact, HE and HIS disciples became so busy attending to their needs, that, they hardly had time to stop and eat. During this time, JESUS' family, who had been tracking HIM, trying to persuade HIM to come home, arrived at the house to try and take HIM back to Nazareth.

Here, we see clearly that JESUS' earthly family, at that time, were not persuaded that JESUS was the MESSIAH, and note in verse 31, that even Mary, JESUS' mother, was with them! Mary and her other sons, James, Joseph, Simon, and Judas (Jude), JESUS' half-brothers (Matthew 13:55), all thought JESUS had lost HIS mind, and had persistently tried to get HIM to come back home with them, because they probably viewed HIM as a family embarrassment.

That is why here in Mark 3, verses 32-35, we see JESUS' seemingly strange reaction and response when HE was informed of their arrival in verse 32. JESUS already knew that HIS earthly family did not believe in HIM. However, it has long been said that "familiarity often breeds contempt", and we see even in JESUS' family of Nazareth, it was apparently no different.

They simply couldn't bring themselves to see, and understand that a person, who had grown up in the same house with them, could ever be even remotely someone as special as that. And the same attitude was prevalent, throughout the city of Nazareth, as we shall see in chapter 6.

And so now we understand more clearly, JESUS' response in verse 33. "Who is my mother? And "Who are my brethren? HE was probably thinking, "Certainly not these people who don't believe me". Then, looking around the room at HIS disciples and all the other people surrounding HIM, who were 100-percent convinced that HE was the MESSIAH, HE says, "These are MY mother and brothers".

In other words, anyone, who does the will of GOD, because they believe in JESUS, the same is HIS family, or, further stated "the children of GOD". Remember, HE was in the world, and the world knew HIM not. In order to come into the family of GOD, one must come out of the world, and to the end of themselves, before they can really get to know, and then believe in, CHRIST JESUS. For it is the will of GOD, that we do so.

## PERSONAL APPLICATION:

(1). Part of JESUS' earthly mission was to separate, or cause "division" among the families of this world (Luke 12:51-53). HE sought to bring the families of the world into the family of GOD. HE already knew that in each earthly family that some would believe, and others wouldn't, even in HIS OWN earthly family, as we saw in this lesson. The only way to come into the family of GOD, is by accepting CHRIST JESUS in your heart. Are you willing to accept JESUS into your heart, so that you can become a member of the family of GOD?

(2). You can't fall in love with anyone, without first, getting to know them. The only way to get to know CHRIST and FATHER GOD is through HIS Holy Scripture. We must seek a personal relationship, or, desire to be related to GOD, on a personal level, through vigorous study of, and obedience to, HIS word.

(3). Make the decision right now to spend more time getting to know GOD, so that you can be adopted into the Holy, eternal family of CHRIST, and then, stick with your decision. Once you accept HIM in your heart, it should be easy to make your residential transition, into the house of GOD.

## LIFE RESPONSE:

Express to GOD, through prayer, that, HE grant you the understanding it takes to realize and take on the character of CHRIST JESUS in your everyday life. Strive to reflect CHRIST' image to others through your daily behavior so that you will also be able to draw others to CHRIST, and thereby, contribute to the growth of the family of GOD.

## KEY VERSE: Mark 3:35

## DEVOTIONAL PASSAGES: John 1:10-12, Luke 12:51-53, Matthew 12:46-50, Mathew 19:29

# LESSON FIVE:

## CALMING THE STORMS
### (Faith in JESUS can and will calm the storms in our lives)

### SCRIPTURE:
### The King James Version
### (Mark 4:35-5:13)

**4 (35)** And the same day, when the even was come, he saith unto them, "Let us pass over unto the other side, **(36)** And when they had sent away the multitude, they took HIM even as HE was in the ship. And there were also with HIM other little ships. **(37)** And there arose a great storm of wind, and the waves beat into the ship, so that it was now full. **(38)** And HE was in the hinder part of the ship, asleep on a pillow: and they awake HIM, and say unto HIM, "MASTER, carest THOU not that we perish?" **(39)** And HE arose, and rebuked the wind, and said unto the sea, "Peace, be still." And the wind ceased, and there was a great calm. **(40)** And HE said unto them, "Why are ye so fearful? How is it that ye have no faith?" **(41)** And they feared exceedingly, and said to one another, "What manner of man is this, that even the wind and the sea obey HIM?

**5 (1)** And they came over unto the other side of the sea, into the country of the Gadarenes. **(2)** And when HE was come out of the ship, immediately there meet HIM out of the tombs a man with an unclean spirit, **(3)** Who had his dwellings among the tombs; and no man could bind him, no, not with chains: **(4)** Because that he had been often bound with fetters and chains, and the chains had been plucked asunder by him, and the fetters broken in pieces: neither could any man tame him. **(5)** And always, night and day, he was in the mountains, and in the tombs, crying, and cutting himself with stones. **(6)** But when he saw JESUS afar off, he ran and worshiped HIM, **(7)** And cried with a loud voice, and said, "What have I to do with THEE, JESUS, THOU SON of the MOST HIGH GOD? I adjure THEE by GOD, that THOU torment me not." **(8)** For HE said unto him, "Come out of the man, thou unclean spirit." **(9)** And HE asked him, "What is thy name?" And he answered, saying, "My name is legion: for we are many." **(10)** And he besought HIM much that HE would not send them away out of the country. **(11)** Now there was there nigh unto the mountains a great herd of swine feeding. **(12)** And all the devils besought HIM, saying, "Send us into the swine, that we may enter into them.  (13) And forth with JESUS gave them leave. And the unclean spirits went out, and entered into the swine: and the herd ran violently down a steep place into the sea, (they were about two thousand;) and were choked in the sea.


COMMENTARY:


In the Greek, the word used for "faith" is "pistis", and it means, "To rely upon with an "inward certainty", and to "assent" to evidence of authority". In the story in Mark chapter 4, verses 35-41, we see something much more than just the calming of a storm at sea. And even though JESUS did, in fact, show mastery over nature, on that stormy evening on the Sea of Galilee, one must stop and show pause to ask, "What does that have to do with us, here in the 21st century?

Well, if we look at this story as just another isolated miracle, we may risk missing its far greater meaning. The eternal meaning in this passage is that, JESUS comes to us to save us, even now, just as HE came to the Disciples, while they were still in the midst of their storm, to save them then. From across the storms of life, HE still comes to those in need, with out-stretched hands, as HE speaks in a calm, clear voice that forever bids us all to "Have no fear".

Here in this passage we see that, wherever JESUS is, the most terrible storms must succumb to HIS overpowering peace. We see, in this story, the Disciples, after realizing the mere presence of JESUS, saw the storm around them become calm, and subside at the very command of the MASTER's voice.

In the ensuing passage in Mark chapter 5, verses 1-13, the story of the man, who was possessed by a group of demons calling themselves "Legion", we see a rather bizarre thing occurring. In order for us to understand this story, we must do our best to read between the lines. It is a story, not unlike many Biblical stories that speak in terms that are quite familiar to the people of those times, but may seem very strange to us in this generation.

First of all, we see that, just as JESUS is climbing out of the boat, a demon-possessed man runs up to HIM and falls to his knees before HIM. Here we see that the demons inside the man recognized JESUS, and then, cried out in fear, saying, "Why are YOU bothering me JESUS, SON of the Most, High GOD? For GOD's sake, do not torture me!"

The demon's name, which is "Legion", gives us a clue as to how many demons may have been present inside the man. "Legion", by definition, was "a Roman regiment consisting of 6000 troops". We also see, subsequently, JESUS casting the demons out of the man, into a herd of two thousand swine, causing them to run down a steep embankment, fall into the sea, and drown. One can only imagine that there must have been quite a storm going on inside of this demon-possessed man.

Also, another lesson to be learned here is how JESUS shows us HIS mastery over satan and his demons. Here we see the demon-possessed man, recognizing the presence of JESUS, and the storm inside of him being made calm with the subsequent release of the demons from his body at the very command of the MASTER's voice.

The lesson to be learned here from these two seemingly very different stories is, that, it doesn't really matter if we are in the storm, like the disciples were in the first story, or the storms of sorrows, problems, and anxiety are in us, like this demon-possessed man in this second story, to recognize GOD as the object of our faith is the key to gaining peace in our lives.

Another thing that we can take away from these passages is that, it doesn't really matter so much what JESUS did on that night, when HE spoke to the sea, "Peace be still", and the winds too, did obey. Nor, does it even matter what JESUS did one morning on a different occasion in far-off Palestine, when HE walked on water, to encourage Peter and those same Disciples (Mark 6:45-52).

What we really need to understand here is that, these miracles present to us a sign and a symbol of what GOD always does for those who have faith, and believe in HIM. And they say, in effect, that, when we are in danger of being overwhelmed by the "storms" of life, GOD will keep in perfect peace, the mind that stays on HIM, because it trusts HIM.

## PERSONAL APPLICATION:

(1). Reflect upon a time, or times when you have felt completely helpless and out control in a life situation. Did you arrive at the conclusion that you need GOD's help, immediately?

(2). Once you had been shaken out of the "illusion of being in control", by your crisis, and reality finally sets in, you probably were able to realize, quite vividly, your lack of trust in the GOD you say you serve.

(3). Next time a crisis hits in your life, let JESUS be your first option, not your last, because, while JESUS is totally capable of handling all the storms that could ever possibly come into your life, HE will not come to your rescue uninvited. We must first ask HIM to get involved and take control of the helm of our lives

LIFE RESPONSE:

Express to GOD, in prayer, your desire to have JESUS take control of the throne of your life, and then, make you into the kind of person that will be humble enough to trust your faith in HIM, not in your own efforts. Pray that GOD will give you the strength, courage, and wisdom to know, to rely only on the promise and character of CHRIST JESUS to steer you safely, through the storms of life.

KEY VERSE: Mark 4:40

DEVOTIONAL PASSAGES: Mark 6:45-52, Matthew 11:28-30, & Exodus 15:2

# LESSON SIX:

(19)

## THE SIGNIFICANCE OF HAVING FAITH
### (Few people reach the level of faith that allows CHRIST to work in their lives)

### SCRIPTURE:
### The King James Version
### (Mark 5:21-43)

**5** **(21)** And when JESUS was passed over again by ship unto the other side, much people gathered unto HIM: and HE was nigh unto the sea. **(22)** And, behold, there cometh one of the rulers of the synagogue, Jairus by name; and when he saw HIM, he fell at HIS feet, **(23)** And besought HIM greatly, saying, "My little daughter lieth at the point of death: I pray thee, come and lay thy hands on her, that she may be healed; and she shall live." **(24)** And JESUS went with him; and much people followed HIM, and thronged HIM. **(25)** And a certain woman, which had an issue of blood twelve years, **(26)** And had suffered many things of many physicians, and had spent all that she had, and was nothing bettered, but rather grew worse, **(27)** When she had heard of JESUS, came in the press behind, and touched HIS garment. **(28)** For she said, "If I may touch but HIS clothes, I shall be whole." **(29)** And straightway the fountain of her blood was dried up; and she felt in her body that she was healed of that plague. **(30)** And JESUS, immediately knowing in HIMSELF that virtue had gone out of HIM, turned HIM about in the press, and said, "Who touched my clothes?" **(31)** And HIS disciples said unto HIM, "THOU seest the multitude thronging THEE, and sayest THOU, Who touched ME?" **(32)** And HE looked round about to see her that had done this thing. **(33)** But the woman fearing and trembling, knowing what was done in her, came and fell down before HIM, and told HIM all the truth. **(34)** And HE said unto her, "Daughter, thy faith has made thee whole; go in peace, and be whole of thy plague." **(35)** While HE yet spake, there came from the ruler of the synagogue's house certain which said, "Thy daughter is dead: why troublest thou the MASTER any further?" **(36)** As soon as JESUS heard the word that was spoken, HE saith unto the ruler of the synagogue, "Be not afraid, only believe." **(37)** And HE suffered no man to follow HIM, save Peter, and James, and John the brother of James. **(38)** And HE cometh to the house of the ruler of the synagogue, and seeth the tumult, and them that wept and wailed greatly. **(39)** And when HE was come in, HE saith unto them, "Why make ye this ado, and weep? The damsel is not dead, but sleepeth." (40) And they laughed HIM to scorn. But when HE had put them all out, HE taketh the father and the mother of the damsel, and them that were with HIM, and entereth in where the damsel was lying. (41) And HE took the damsel by the hand, and said unto her, "Talitha cumi"; which is being interpreted, "Damsel, I say unto thee, arise." (42) And straightway the damsel arose, and walked; for she was of the age of twelve years. And they were astonished with a great astonishment. (43) And HE charged them straitly that no man should know it; and commanded that something should be given her to eat.


COMMENTARY:


William Barclay once wrote, "The greatness of JESUS was that HE was prepared to pay the price of helping others, and that price was the outgoing of HIS very life. We follow in HIS footsteps only when we are prepared to spend, not only our substance, but our souls and strength for others".

Old Testament prophets, such as Isaiah, prophesied that JESUS would have power to bring back wholeness of life. And we can see clearly, here in these passages, and, in fact, throughout JESUS' ministry, HIM demonstrating that power, time and time again.

In Mark chapter 5, verses 21-43, John Mark gives us two vivid descriptions of remarkable cases where JESUS demonstrates HIS restoration powers for all to see. However, in the story of the woman with the issue of blood, he shows us perhaps, the most vivid example in scripture of how, when JESUS healed someone, it quite literally, drained the life right out of HIM. In other words, every time JESUS healed someone, little by little, HE spent HIS very life to do it.

It is a penetrating thought, because, we as human beings, often do not stop to consider when we receive help from others, just how much it may have cost that person in order to provide us with that kindness, or largesse. When we look at JESUS' ministry in that light, it somehow seems to show us a whole new, even more lovely side, to an already, incredibly lovely story.

But first, we see a man named Jairus, a Synagogue Ruler, come to JESUS to ask for help for his dying daughter. Jairus, just from the standpoint of the position that he held in the synagogue, most likely, did not have an outpouring of love in his heart for JESUS up unto this point. For, he was not just an ordinary employee of the synagogue, but in fact, was a Phariscc, or leader in the synagogue.

In fact, in order to hold the position that he held, he not only must have been a devout orthodox Jew, one of JESUS' strongest opponents, but also, he had to be the head of the Board of Elders, one of the requirements of holding the position of "ruler". And so we can now imagine how much pride Jairus must have had to swallow, before he could come seeking the help of the opposition, JESUS.

Truly this must have been a last ditch, desperate attempt to try and save his twelve-year old daughter's life. GOD had apparently used this man's love for his child to help him overcome whatever differences he may have had toward the man, JESUS, WHOM he had heard so much about. He was now willing and able to turn his feelings of religious bias, into a small measure of "saving faith" that would bring restoration, and salvation, to his daughter' life, as well as his own.

Jairus was now able to come to the end of himself (something we all have to do if we ever expect to see JESUS), in order that he might save his daughter's life, through his faith in what JESUS could do for him. And perhaps through his close scrutiny of JESUS' life, he now believed and possessed enough faith that JESUS truly was the SON of the living GOD.

In the story that is sandwiched in between the beginning and ending of Jairus' story of new-found faith (Vs.24-34), we see the compelling account of the lady known to us only as the "woman with the issue of blood". John Mark tells us that this particular woman had been hemorrhaging for twelve years, and she too, had come to JESUS as a last resort. She had suffered through many doctors for many years, spent all of her money, and in the end, had only gotten worse.

By the time she heard of JESUS, she had very little faith left for anything, or anyone. In fact, she even seems to approach JESUS to touch the hem of HIS garment in a very suspicious, even superstitious manner, perhaps as if one would touch a prayer cloth.

However, even a little faith in JESUS can bring a lot of changes and improvements to the lives of even the most defeated among us. So the lady cast the last vestiges of her faith and hope in the direction of CHRIST JESUS, and she received, as a result, more healing than all of her money could buy her over a twelve-year period. And JESUS' only charge to her was that she, "go in peace".

And so, in both these stories, we see a very loving, and lasting thought emerge. It is a thought, we can all, certainly come to rest in, when we feel we're ready to let CHRIST take over the thrones of our lives. It is the thought that, we don't have to wait until our motives, or faith is perfect, before we come to HIM. The only thing that really matters is that we do come.

Remember, JESUS has never healed, or given salvation to a "perfect" man, or woman. Every one of us needs JESUS, because of our imperfections. In both of these stories we can see, quite vividly, that JESUS is willing to accept us as we are, and then, is able to make us what we ought to be. HE simply shows us how to obtain eternal life, through faith in HIM.

### PERSONAL APPLICATION:

(1). It is quite typical for the average person to exhibit little faith in CHRIST, in the beginning. But as we grow in CHRIST, HE expects our faith in HIM to also grow. Have you ever asked GOD to confirm HIS will, through a sign? If so, after receiving the sign, did it strengthen your faith and belief in HIM?

(2). Make you a scale, and number it one to ten. Circle the number where you think your faith was when you first came to CHRIST. Now circle the number where you think your faith is now. Then, circle the number where you would like for your faith to be.

(3). If it is not a ten, then set the goal of getting to know CHRIST better through the word of GOD. Next, try trusting CHRIST by stepping out in faith in your obedience to the word of GOD. And finally, become a persistent doer of the word of GOD, and before long, you'll find the number on your scale of faith has moved up considerably, even to where it ought to be.

### LIFE RESPONSE

Pray a prayer of thanks to GOD for HIS patience with your inadequate faith, and that HE continues to challenge you with new ways to serve HIM that will fortify your faith in HIM, throughout your Christian walk.

### KEY VERSE: Mark 5:36

### DEVOTIONAL PASSAGES: Luke 17:5-6, John 14:1-6, Hebrews 11

# LESSON SEVEN:

(23)

## REJECTION AND MISSION
### (CHRIST'S message can offend, or empower)

## SCRIPTURE:
**The King James Version**
**(Mark 6:1-13)**

**6** (1) And HE went out from thence, and came into HIS own country; and HIS disciples follow HIM. (2) And when the sabbath day was come, HE began to teach in the synagogue: and many hearing HIM were astonished, saying, "From whence hath THIS MAN these things? and what wisdom is this which is given unto HIM, that even such mighty works are wrought by HIS hands? (3) Is not THIS THE CARPENTER, THE SON of Mary, THE BROTHER of James, and Joses, and of Juda, and Simon? and are not HIS sisters here with us?" And they were offended at HIM. (4) But JESUS said unto them, "A prophet is not without honour, but in his own country, and among his own kin, and in his own house". (5) And HE could there do no mighty work, save that HE laid HIS hands upon a few sick folk, and healed them. (6) And HE marvelled because of their unbelief. And HE went round about the villages, teaching. (7) And HE called unto HIM the twelve, and began to send them forth by two and two; and gave them power over unclean spirits; (8) And commanded them that they should take nothing for their journey, save a staff only; no scrip, no bread, no money in their purse: (9) But be shod with sandals; and not put on two coats. (10) And HE said unto them, "In what place soever ye enter into an house, there abide till ye depart from that place. (11) And whosoever shall not receive you, nor hear you, when ye depart thence, shake off the dust under your feet for a testimony against them. Verily I say unto you, it shall be more tolerable for Sodom and Gomorrha in the day of judgment, than for that city". (12) And they went out, and preached that men should repent. (13) And they cast out many devils, and anointed with oil many that were sick, and healed them.

## COMMENTARY:

**M**ark chapter 6 contains five of the most familiar events of JESUS' ministry. This perhaps, makes it also one the most dramatic chapters in all of Scripture. Here in this chapter, we see first, JESUS being rejected, in HIS own hometown of Nazareth (Vs.1-6).

Next we see HIS empowerment of HIS original Disciples to Preach and Teach, and cast out Demons for the very first time (v.7-13). We also see the death of John the Baptist (v.14-29), and the miraculous feeding of the 5000 men with five loaves of bread, and two fish (v.30-44). And finally, we see this famous chapter being brought to a close, with John Mark's vivid description of JESUS' now legendary, "walk on water". But let us now just focus on the first two events of this chapter.

When JESUS first came back to Nazareth after beginning HIS ministry, HE was not exactly treated as a favorite son of the community. It is often said that there is never a more severe critic of anyone, than those who have known you all of your life. And unfortunately for the Nazarenes, they greeted JESUS' teachings with contempt, and took offense to HIS even coming there.

However, familiarity often breeds contempt, and that surely was the case here in JESUS' hometown of Nazareth. They refused to listen to JESUS that day, perhaps, for two very human and ungodly reasons. First of all, in their minds, JESUS was just a carpenter, a working man, just like them. And secondly, JESUS had grown up right there in Nazareth, before their eyes, and they couldn't make the leap that HE could be anybody, even remotely special, or important. Isn't that, pretty much, the same way we treat those familiar to us today?

There can be no teaching, or preaching in the wrong atmosphere, and on that day in Nazareth, the atmosphere was clearly wrong. A person can never be healed, if they refuse to accept the treatment necessary, to make it so. They must, first and foremost, at least be receptive to what is being offered.

On that day, JESUS was really seeking to prepare HIS Disciples for the rejection that they themselves would soon face, and HE told them just how they should handle it when HE sent them out on their first mission as HIS chosen few (verse 11). HE instructed them that day that, if any place would not offer hospitality, or listen to their message, they were to leave that place, and shake, even the dust from that place, off their feet.

JESUS also goes on, to tell them this, "Verily I say unto you, it shall be more tolerable for Sodom and Gomorrah in the Day of Judgment, than for the city that rejects their teaching". No doubt this statement provokes serious thought, and perhaps leads to repentance by some who have rejected GOD's Word in the past.

This story serves to remind us, that, sometimes we can be too close to a person to see their greatness. When we look at people, remember too, that no one is outside the purpose of GOD. One never knows, who, GOD may be using for HIS mighty purpose. We only need to be able to recognize the things of GOD, when we hear, and see them, and then, make the decision to help, rather than hinder, in the work of CHRIST.

## PERSONAL APPLICATION:

(1). Did you reject the Gospel the first time you heard it, or, did you welcome it as a refreshing, eye-opening experience?

(2). Consider this; by rejecting JESUS, the people of Nazareth forfeited a chance at eternal joy in Heaven. After being around JESUS virtually all of HIS life on this earth, HIS family, and the people of Nazareth failed to recognize HIS greatness. Don't let the familiarity of people around you, breed contempt in your acceptance of the fact that GOD can use anyone to do HIS righteous bidding. And, always remember that, no one is outside of the purpose of the ALMIGHTY GOD.

(3). As you learn and grow in CHRIST, work hard to prepare yourself for the challenges that you will surely face when you began to carry out the great commission of CHRIST, which is spreading HIS Gospel to all who will accept it, anywhere in the world.

## LIFE RESPONSE:

Pray and ask GOD to give you the strength and courage to continue to share the Gospel with dignity and respect, despite whatever rejection to HIS word that you may encounter. Ask that HE empower you with the SPIRIT, and then, go before you and prepare the hearts of those, to whom you may be speaking. Finally, ask that HE continue to help you to suffer for the faith in CHRIST that you hold, in order that you may always recognize its value, and keep it in the proper perspective.

KEY VERSE: Mark 6:4

DEVOTIONAL PASSAGES: Mark 3:21, John 7:37-52, Matthew 10:37-42

# LESSON EIGHT:

(26)

## A LITTLE IS A LOT IN THE HANDS OF JESUS
(JESUS can supply the needs of those who hunger for HIM)

### SCRIPTURE:
The King James Version
(Mark 6:34-44)

**6** (34) And JESUS, when HE came out, saw much people, and was moved with compassion toward them, because they were as sheep not having a shepherd: and HE began to teach them many things. (35) And when the day was now far spent, HIS disciples came unto HIM, and said, "This is a desert place, and now the time is far passed: (36) Send them away, that they may go into the country round about, and into the villages, and buy themselves bread: for they have nothing to eat." (37) HE answered and said unto them, "Give ye them to eat." And they say unto HIM, "Shall we go and buy two hundred pennyworth of bread, and give them to eat?" (38) HE saith unto them, "How many loaves have ye? Go and see." And when they knew, they say, "Five, and two fishes." (39) And HE commanded them to make all sit down by companies upon the green grass. (40) And they sat down in ranks, by hundreds, and by fifties. (41) And when HE had taken the five loaves and the two fishes, HE looked up to Heaven, and blessed, and brake the loaves, and gave them to HIS disciples to set before them; and the two fishes divided HE among them all. (42) And they did all eat, and were filled. (43) And they took up twelve baskets full of the fragments, and the fishes. (44) And they that did eat of the loaves were about five thousand men.

## COMMENTARY:

The significance of the story of the feeding of the five thousand is demonstrated in its deliberate introduction, and, in the fact that JESUS refers back to this event twice (Mark 6:52 & 8:17-21). Then too, it is the only event, other than the resurrection, that is mentioned by the writers of all four of the Gospels.

This event's importance lies in the fact that it illustrates the compassion of JESUS for the hungry. It also illustrates how badly JESUS wanted to drive home the importance to HIS disciples to not only be concerned about the hungry, but to also take action to remedy their condition even though their own financial standing, or resources may seem to be limited at the time. This story also serves to show us, that, our belief in JESUS can multiply our resources, if, we are willing to commit ourselves to HIS service.

In reading this passage, we can clearly see that it reads exactly like an eye-witness account. Yet, we already know that John Mark is writing down the Apostle Peter's recollections of his time spent with JESUS, during HIS three-year earthbound mission.

Nevertheless, the description here in this passage by Mark, is remarkably clear. His description of the green grass, for example, tells us that this event most likely occurred in the late spring, the only time of year, in that area, where this condition usually exists.

It was also, probably, in the late afternoon, since the sun then sets at around six o'clock p.m. We also get a pretty good mental picture of the way the people were told to sit on the ground in sections of fifty and a hundred. And we can see that, even in this, JESUS demanded decency and order. And finally, we see JESUS looking to HIS FATHER GOD to add a blessing on the food that they were about to receive into their bodies.

When we rely on JESUS, all things become possible, and it becomes impossible for us not to succeed in all of our GODly endeavors. In this story we see two very different reactions to the human need, that of the disciples, and, that of JESUS. The disciples wanted to send the needs of the people away, into the hands of someone other than themselves. JESUS' response to HIS disciples was "You feed them".

The world is full of people who want to pass the problems of their fellowman on to someone else. But there is an obvious shortage of people in the world who say, "It is I, myself, who must take the responsibility of helping my brother and sister with their needs".


PERSONAL APPLICATION:

(1). The personal application here is clear. It is embodied in the oldest
commandment of the Christian Doctrine, and it is also the second of the
greatest, most important commandments, period. That command simply
states that we, "Love your neighbor as yourself" (Matthew 22:37-40).

(2). Don't pass the needs of your neighbor on to someone else, unless you are
     sure you are helping them by doing so. But otherwise, you should help them.
(3). Learn to rely on the wisdom of the LORD to help you to help others.

## LIFE RESPONSE:

Pray to GOD to give you the wisdom and resources, so that you will always be
prepared to help others when the need arises. And then, ask that HE test you, by
giving you the opportunities to do so, and finally, ask HIM to give you the faith,
courage, and compassion needed to pass that test.

## KEY VERSE: Mark 6:37

## DEVOTIONAL PASSAGES: Matthew 14:13-21, Luke 9:10-17, John 6:1-15

# LESSON NINE:

## WHAT REALLY DEFILES
### (Mere actions are not a substitute for a GODly attitude)

### SCRIPTURE:
#### The King James Version
#### (Mark 7:1-16)

**7** **(1)** Then came together unto HIM the Pharisees, and certain of the scribes, which came from Jerusalem. **(14)** And when they saw some of HIS disciples eat bread with defiled, that is to say, with unwashen, hands, they found fault. **(3)** For the Pharisees, and all the Jews, except they wash their hand oft, eat not, holding the tradition of the elders. **(4)** And when they come from the market, except they wash, they eat not. And many other things there be, which they have received to hold, as the washing of cups, and pots, brasen vessels, and tables. **(5)** Then the Pharisees and scribes asked HIM, "Why walk not thy disciples according to the tradition of the elders, but eat bread with unwashen hands?" **(6)** HE answered and said unto them, "Well hath Esaias prophesied of you hypocrites, as it is written, This people honoreth me with their lips, but their heart is far from ME.

**(7)** Howbeit in vain do they worship ME, teaching for doctrines the commandments of men. **(8)** For laying aside the commandment of GOD, ye hold the tradition of men, as the washing of pots and cups: and many other such like things ye do." **(9)** And HE said unto them, "Full well ye reject the commandment of GOD, that ye may keep your own tradition.

**(10)** For Moses said, Honour thy father and thy mother; and, whoso curseth father or mother, let him die the death: **(11)** But ye say, if a man shall say to his father or mother, it is corban, that is to say, a gift, by whatsoever thou mightest be profited by me; he shall be free. **(12)** And ye suffer him no more to do ought for his father or his mother; **(13)** Making the word of GOD of none effect through your tradition, which ye have delivered: and many such like things do ye." **(14)** And when HE had called all the people unto HIM, HE said unto them, "Hearken unto me every one of you, and understand: **(15)** There is nothing from without a man, that entering into him can defile him: but the things which come out of him, those are they that defile the man. **(16)** If any man have ears to hear, let him hear."

## COMMENTARY:

In Mark chapter 7, verses 1-16, we begin to see vivid examples of the core differences between JESUS, and the Pharisees and Scribes of HIS day. For the Orthodox Jew, the Law meant two things. First of all, it meant the "Ten Commandments". Secondly, it meant the first five books of the Old Testament, otherwise known as the "Pentateuch".

From these two Documents, they formed a very complex, self-made, spoken list of rules and regulations, known as "Oral Law", or "The Traditions of the Elders". Roughly three hundred years after the Crucifixion of CHRIST, these Oral Laws were written down for the very first time. Today they form the compilation we know as, the "Mishnah".

There are two aspects of these "Scribal rules and regulations" that come into play in this particular passage of Scripture. In verse two, John Mark uses the Greek word "koinos" (koy-nos) in his original writings, and it means "ceremonially unclean and unfit for the service and worship of GOD". This is regarding the "hand washing" rituals practiced by the Jews, and, that is talked about here in this passage. Then there is also the ritual of completely immersing ones hands in water, and washing down any merchandise bought at the Marketplace, for fear that a "Gentile", or unclean person may have touched them.

And so, to the Scribes and the Pharisees, these unwritten rules and regulations made up the very essence of their Religion. In their minds, they were pleasing GOD by performing these ritual. However, in the spiritual sense, JESUS and these people were miles apart in their thinking, and here in this passage we see the fundamental contrast between the man, who sees religion as ritual, and the man, who sees in religion, loving GOD, and loving his fellowman.

In verse six, in JESUS' response to these religious leaders regarding their questions of uncleanness, HE accuses them of basically two things. First of all, HE accuses them of "hypocrisy". In John Mark's original writings, he uses the Greek word "Hupokrites" (Hoop-ok-ree-tace). It is a word that describes "one whose whole life is a piece of acting, without even a trace of sincerity". It is from this word that we derive our English word "Hypocrite".

Secondly, JESUS accuses them of "substituting the Laws of GOD", with the "efforts of man's Human ingenuity" (i.e. Christian denominations), or, in other words, using their own "man-made" rules, regulations, and observances, apart from the Christian Bible, in their various churches.

The cleverness of men can never be the basis of true Religion, and true Religion can never be produced in the recesses of the impure minds of men. Christianity, is the only "True Religion", simply because, it is the only religion that is a product of the mind of GOD. It is based solely on simply listening to, and accepting the word of GOD, by Faith. We must be forever cognizant of the fact that, any rule that prevents us from helping our fellowman, has never been, is not now, and will never be, a rule of GOD's.

In verse eleven, we see the use of the Greek word "Corban", and it is "a gift or offering that is earmarked for GOD, and is not subject to human use". Oddly, this is the only time that this word is used in Scripture. In those days, if a person didn't want to share something with another person, they would simply claim that it is "Corban". Here, JESUS is giving an example of how human ingenuity is used to "get around" obeying the Word of GOD, or making the Word of GOD "of none effect" in one's life.

There were many differences between JESUS and these so-called Religious Leaders, and these Leaders were clearly wrong. It is an undeniable fact, that, man did not know who GOD was, until JESUS came along. Before that, man believed that worshiping GOD, in effect, was done, from the "outside in". However, JESUS came to show us that worshiping GOD is done, from the "inside out".

In verse 15, JESUS says that we are not defiled by anything that comes from without, nor, from anything that we eat. A person can only be defiled by what they "say, and do", and with that said, I guest that really means, that our whole lives, should really be declared "Corban" for GOD.

## PERSONAL APPLICATION:

(1) While the religious leaders of JESUS' day knew the Scriptures inside and out as far as the letter of the Law goes, spiritually, they knew nothing of GOD at all. As a result, somewhere down the line, they began to replace the laws of GOD with their own rules and regulations. As we increase our knowledge of GOD, be careful not to let the power that comes with it, pull you out of the will of GOD, especially, in the form of self-consuming pride, arrogance and self-righteousness.

(2) It is important that we learn to worship GOD in spirit, and in truth, and that way, the more we get to know HIM, the more we respect, honor, love, and have faith in HIM, and not in ourselves.

(3) Faith, Hope, and Love are the three great enduring things, and of the three,

Love is the greatest, Faith and Hope are only mere manifestations of Love, but because of it, they too will endure forever. To tell the truth, without love, can result in great potential damage, because, truth without love is usually accompanied, by bad motives.


## LIFE RESPONSE:


Pray to GOD for forgiveness of trying to serve HIM in deeds, and not with purity of heart, with knowledge, and not with spirit and love. Ask GOD to help you to turn over a new leaf in service of HIM, and, that you be more able to worship HIM in spirit and in truth, from this day forward.


KEY VERSE: Mark 7:15

DEVOTIONAL PASSAGES: Luke 6:37-42, Colossians 2:6-10, Psalm 51:10-17

# LESSON TEN:

(33)

## JESUS: A GOOD THAT IS ALSO LOVELY
### (Longsuffering and intercession)

### SCRIPTURE:
**The King James Version**
**(Mark 7:24-37)**

**7 (24)** And from thence HE arose, and went into the borders of Tyre and Sidon, and entered into an house, and would have no man know it: but HE could not be hid. **(25)** For a certain woman, whose young daughter had an unclean spirit, heard of HIM, and came and fell at HIS feet: **(26)** The woman was a Greek, a Syro-phenician by nation; and she besought HIM that HE would cast forth the devil out of her daughter. **(27)** But JESUS said unto her, "Let the children first be filled: for it is not meet to take the children's bread, and to cast it unto the dogs." **(28)** And she answered and said unto HIM, "Yes, LORD: yet the dogs under the table eat of the children's crumbs. **(29)** And HE said unto her, "For this saying go thy way; the devil is gone out of thy daughter." **(30)** And when she was come to her house, she found the devil gone out, and her daughter laid upon the bed. **(31)** And again, departing from the coasts of Tyre and Sidon, HE came unto the Sea of Galilee, through the midst of the coasts of Decapolis. **(32)** And they bring unto HIM one that was deaf, and had an impediment in his speech; and they beseech HIM to put HIS hand upon him. **(33)** And HE took him aside from the multitude, and put HIS fingers into his ears, and HE spit, and touched his tongue; **(34)** And looking up to Heaven, HE sighed, and saith unto him, "Ephphatha", that is, Be opened. **(35)** And straightway his ears were opened, and the string of his tongue was loosed, and he spake plain. **(36)** And HE charged them that they should tell no man: but the more HE charged them, so much the more a great deal they published it; **(37)** And were beyond measure astonished, saying, HE hath done all things well: HE maketh both the deaf to hear, and the dumb to speak.

## COMMENTARY:

In the Greek, the word used for "longsuffering" is "makrothumia", and it "describes a spirit that never grows irritated, never despairs", and particularly, in this lesson, "never regards anyone as being beyond salvation".

In Mark chapter 7, verses 24-30, in the story of the Syro-Phoenician woman, who was also a Canaanite, one of the most hated enemies of the Jews in those days, JESUS shows his disciples, by healing this Gentile's woman's daughter, because of her faith, that the Gospel would be embraced by both Jews and Gentiles alike.

Here JESUS sought to show HIS disciples then, and us now, that, prayer is made for all men, and that, for the Christian, there would be no such thing as an enemy, except satan, in all the world. HE wanted it to be understood that, no one is outside of the love of CHRIST, and no one is outside of the purpose of GOD. GOD wants all people to be saved.

In 1 Timothy 2:1, the word Paul uses for "intercession", in his original Greek writing, is "enteuxis" (ent-yook-sis), and it means "to enter into the presence of a king, in order to present a petition on behalf of someone else". Now that tells us a lot about the power of prayer, but most of all, it tells us that the way to GOD is always open through prayer, even and especially, to petition unselfishly for someone else. When we pray intercessory prayers we usher someone else into the presence of the Almighty GOD.

In the ensuing story, here in Mark chapter 7, verses 31-37, John Mark gives us a vivid description, of just such a case, of "intercession". There, we see the friends of a deaf and dumb man, bring him into the presence of JESUS, in order to petition that JESUS might heal him. It's a lovely story really, because here we see a man with a special need, and a special problem. And so here JESUS applies the, most tender, of considerations, as HE spares the man of his feeling of embarrassment by pulling him aside, away from the crowd.

After completion of this miracle healing, the people declared that JESUS "had done all things well". Ironically, this is very reminiscent of what is said of GOD, in Genesis 1:31, after HE had completed creation of the Heaven and the Earth. There it says, "GOD saw everything that HE had made, and, behold, "it was very good" (KJV).

When JESUS came to usher in the re-generating "New Covenant", HE, in effect, was beginning the work of creation all over again. In the beginning, all things had been made good by HIS FATHER, however, the sins of man had, in time, ruined it all. And now we see here, and, throughout JESUS' ministry, HIM bringing back the beauty of GOD, to a world, that the sins of man had already, long ago, rendered ugly.

Old Testament prophets, such as Isaiah, predicted that the MESSIAH would have power to "bring back wholeness of life", and clearly, when JESUS came to earth HE demonstrated that power, time and time again. And so, now, we see yet two more ways as to how we can love and care for our fellowman, through the example of JESUS. It is first by, "longsuffering" ("makrothumia"), putting up with each other's weaknesses, because we all have them. And secondly, by "intercession" ("enteuxis"), interceding for someone, who for mental, physical, or spiritual reasons may not be able to "petition", or "pray" for themselves.

In the biblical Greek there are two words that are used for "good". One is "agathos", and it is a good, as in being a "good person". The other is "kalos", and it describes a good that is also "lovely". kalos is the kind of good that describes JESUS CHRIST, and, it is this kind of good, that describes GOD's, and JESUS', attitude towards helping mankind, HIS greatest creation, and the only part of HIS creation who are made in HIS "spiritual image".

We see here in, both of these stories, JESUS' "good", that is also "lovely". When we see HIS power, and, HIS sensitivity, we see a good that is also, lovely. When we see HIS authority, and, HIS gentleness, we see a good that is also, lovely. And finally, when we see HIS majesty, and, HIS kindness, we can't help but see "a good" that is also "lovely".

## PERSONAL APPLICATION:

(1). In both these stories we see that, because of others showing concern for someone other than themselves, they were able to evoke the immediate compassion of JESUS. Whenever we intercede for others, we demonstrate to JESUS, just how much we love and care for our neighbor.

(2). It didn't matter to JESUS, that the woman in the first story was Gentile, HIS compassion extends to all people, who believe in HIM. Train yourself to be "longsuffering" with all people, because it is possible for anyone to become a child of GOD, by receiving CHRIST's salvation.

(3). Next time you encounter a person, whom you do not know, who has a prayer concern, show compassion by offering to intercede in prayer for that person. It would be doing a "good thing" that is also "lovely".

## LIFE RESPONSE:

Pray a petition to GOD for HIS help with specific people, whom you feel are a burden on your emotions, because they can't seem to get their life together, and yet, are not willing to commit themselves to CHRIST. Then, thank HIM for always being there to listen to our concerns for others, as well as ourselves, and answering those prayers in a way that is most beneficial to us.

**KEY VERSE: Mark 7:37**

**DEVOTIONAL PASSAGES: Mark 2:1-12, Luke 7:1-10, Matthew 9:18-26**

## LESSON ELEVEN:

## AFFIRMATION AND CONFESSION OF FAITH
(Who do you say that HE is?)

### SCRIPTURE:
The King James Version
(Mark 8:27-30 & 9:2-7)

**8** **(27)** And JESUS went out, and HIS disciples, into the towns of Caesarea Philippi: and by the way HE asked HIS disciples, saying unto them, "Whom do men say that I am?" **(28)** And they answered, "John the Baptist: but some say, Elias; and others, One of the prophets." **(29)** And HE saith unto them, "But whom say ye that I am?" And Peter answered and saith unto HIM, "THOU art the CHRIST." **(30)** And HE charged them that they should tell no man of HIM.

**9** **(2)** And after six days JESUS taketh with HIM Peter, and James, and John, and leadeth them up into an high mountain apart by themselves: and HE was transfigured before them. **(3)** And HIS raiment became shining, exceeding white as snow; so as no fuller on earth can white them. **(4)** And there appeared unto them Elias with Moses: and they were talking with JESUS. **(5)** And Peter answered and said to JESUS, "MASTER, it is good for us to be here: and let us make three tabernacles; one for THEE, and one for Moses, and one for Elias." **(6)** For he wist not what to say; for they were sore afraid. **(7)** And there was a cloud that overshadowed them: and a voice came out of the cloud, saying, "This is MY beloved SON: hear HIM."

### COMMENTARY:

In Mark 8:27-30, John Mark writes of the 25-mile walk, of JESUS and HIS Disciples, from Galilee to Caesarea-Philippi. Now it is no accident that JESUS chose this particular time and area to pose the question to the Disciples, "Who do men say that I am?" And subsequently, "Who do you say that I am?"

At that time, Caesarea-Philippi was notorious for "idol worship". In fact, it was a "mecca" of various religions, as there were no less than fourteen temples of idol worship in this immediate vicinity. All of the Syrian Gods got their worship there, and so did many others.

In addition, there was a mountain in Caesarea-Philippi that contained a deep cavern that was said to be the birthplace of "Pan", the "Greek God of Nature". In fact, Pan is the source of Caesarea-Philippi's former name of "Paneas", which was changed to "Caesarea-Philippi", by "Philip the Tetrarch", who was the son of "Herod the Great", in honor of Caesar Augustus.

Herod the Great had also constructed a huge white marble tower, that was the most imposing edifice in Caesarea-Philippi in those days, and he dedicated it to Caesar also, because, Caesar too, was considered to be a God at that time.

Caesarea-Philippi is also the place where the Jordan River begins. We all know of the Jordan River, as it is the place where John the Baptist did most of his baptizing. In fact, he even baptized JESUS there, at the beginning of HIS earthly ministry.

And so, it is against this backdrop of Greek and Syrian Gods, this place where the history of Israel also dominates men' minds, that we see JESUS, the carpenter's son from Nazareth, stand and pose the question to HIS disciples, "Who do men say that I am?"

Here JESUS sets HIMSELF against the backdrop of the world's most prominent religions, in all their history and splendor, and demands to be compared to them by HIS disciples, and fully expect the verdict to be handed down in HIS favor! Nowhere else in Scripture does JESUS' awareness, of HIS own deity shine through, with a, more clear and dazzling light.

In the Greek, the word used for "affirmation" is "bebaiosis" (beb-ah-yo-sis), and it means "to be steadfast and sure in one's assertions". When Peter pondered this question from JESUS, he knew that all human categories would ultimately fail to describe, just who JESUS was.

This particular passage serves to show us that our discovery of JESUS must be "a personal discovery". Remember, JESUS also in this passage, asks the question, "Who do Y-O-U say that I am? It hints that our knowledge of JESUS must never be "secondhand", but rather, our relationship must be a personal, experiential one.

Christianity does not consist of just, "knowing about JESUS", it consists of "knowing JESUS personally and spiritually". JESUS always demands "a personal verdict" in one's determination of who we believe HE is. And when JESUS asked this question, HE was not just asking it Peter and HIS other Disciples. It is also a question that comes to us, from across the spans of time, in hopes that we too can answer it favorably.

JESUS' "Transfiguration" (Mark 9:1-10), which in all geographical likelihood, occurred on Mt. Hermon nearly 2000 years ago, was mcant to place "Affirmation" of JESUS' majesty, on the hearts of men. GOD spoke from the clouds that day to

Peter, James and John, to forever affirm, that JESUS truly is HIS only begotten SON.

And HE used the images of Moses and Elijah, the Law and the Prophet, two towering figures in Jewish history, each, of whom, no man had seen die. But they were there, nevertheless, to bear witness, and add affirmation to this divine event. And as for Peter, James and John, they, in a very special sense, had become witnesses to the glory of CHRIST. And now, they had the story of that glory embedded in their hearts, so that they may go out and tell all men, that JESUS truly is the SON of the living GOD.

We may never be able to witness an event such as the one that occurred on a mountaintop overlooking Caesarea-Philippi that day.  But certainly, we can follow the instructions of JESUS, as they were laid down to HIS disciples, particularly in John 21. If we love JESUS, each of us can help someone else guard against going astray. And if we love JESUS, each of us can love one another. And, if we love JESUS, each of us is surely capable of feeding HIS sheep, with the nourishing food, of the word of GOD.

## PERSONAL APPLICATION:

(1). Are you truly persuaded that JESUS is the CHRIST? If so, what persuaded you?

(2). Many of us have known who JESUS is for most of our lives, and some have even put their trust in HIM, as their LORD and SAVIOR. However, the world of today is constantly pushing us to believe that JESUS is something less than HE really is, the SON of the ONLY WISE GOD. When JESUS is allowed to enter into the hearts of men, with it, comes affirmation of HIS majesty in our minds and souls. Open up your spiritual heart, and let JESUS come in and abide.

(3). Identify ways by which you feel you know who JESUS is, and then, write them down and share them with someone, who may be struggling with their unbelief.

## LIFE RESPONSE:

Pray a prayer of thanks to GOD and praise HIM for sending HIS only begotten SON, so that we, as undeserving as we are, might come to know HIM, love HIM, and glorify HIM forever.

KEY VERSE: Mark 8:29

DEVOTIONAL PASSAGES: John 6:64-69, Philippians 2:5-11, Romans 10:5-13

# LESSON TWELVE:

## HONEST FAITH
### (Overcoming moments of unbelief)

## SCRIPTURE:
### The King James Version
### (Mark (9:14-29)

**9** (14) And when HE came to HIS disciples, HE saw a great multitude about them, and the scribes questioning with them. (15) And straightway all the people, when they beheld HIM, were greatly amazed, and running to HIM saluted HIM. (16) And HE asked the scribes, "What question ye with them?" (17) And one of the multitude answered and said, "MASTER, I have brought unto THEE my son, which hath a dumb spirit; (18) And wheresoever he taketh him, he teareth him: and he foameth, and gnasheth with his teeth, and pineth away: and I spake to THY disciples that they should cast him out; and they could not." (19) HE answereth him, and saith, "O faithless generation, how long shall I be with you? How long shall I suffer you? bring him unto ME. (20) And they brought him unto HIM: and when HE saw him, straightway the spirit tare him; and he fell on the ground, and wallowed foaming. (21) And HE asked his father, "How long is it ago since this came unto him?" and he said, "of a child". (22) And oftimes it has cast him into the fire, and into the waters, to destroy him: but if THY canst do anything, have compassion on us, and help us. (23) JESUS said unto him, "If thou canst believe, all things are possible to him that believeth". (24) And straightway the father of the child cried out, and said with tears, "LORD, I believe; help THOU mine unbelief". (25) When JESUS saw that the people came running together, HE rebuked the foul spirit, saying unto him, "thou dumb and deaf spirit, I charge thee, come out of him, and enter no more into him." (26) And the spirit cried, and rent him sore, and came out of him: and he was as one dead; insomuch that many said, "He is dead". (27) But JESUS took him by the hand, and lifted him up; and he arose. (28) And when HE was come into the house, HIS disciples asked HIM privately, "Why could not we cast him out? (29) And HE said unto them, "This kind can come forth by nothing, but by prayer and fasting"

## COMMENTARY:

In Mark chapter 9, verses 14-18, John Mark gives us an account of an argument involving the Scribes and some of JESUS' disciples, as the Scribes take advantage of their inability to cast out a Demon from a little boy. The Scribes, no doubt, were seeking to use this incident, to try and deflect the ineptitude of JESUS' Disciples, onto JESUS' reputation as their leader.

Here we see that, no sooner than JESUS, Peter, James, and John had come down from Mt. Hermon following JESUS' Transfiguration, they encounter this controversy brewing between the Disciples and the Scribes.

This gives us an opportunity to see how JESUS is not only ready to face HIS impending death on the cross, but also, how HE had to remain ready to tackle the problems of the World that lay all along HIS journey, before HE even got to the cross. However, one of JESUS' gifts was that HE possessed a characteristic that allowed HIM to be able to give of HIMSELF, entirely, to each individual that HE happened to come in contact with.

In Mark 9:19-24, we see how JESUS chose to handle this hot controversy. First, HE tells them to "Bring the boy unto me". Then, JESUS states to the boy's father, the condition, upon which all miracles must hinge. HE tells him, "To him that believes, all things, are possible".

In the Greek, the word used for faith is "pistis", and it means to "rely upon with an "inward certainty", and to "assent" to evidence of authority". We see here that these people, including the Disciples, had not yet began to rely upon JESUS, with an inward certainty, and had not yet assented to all the evidence they had seen of JESUS' authority.

However, instead of JESUS sitting around waiting on the worldly thinking of these men to catch up, HE chose to go ahead and deal with the situation of healing the child right away. JESUS then commanded the "spirit of deafness and muteness" to come out of the child and never return, and the evil spirit did obey.

Sometimes, as in the case of the boy's father, we tend to get less than we expect from the professed Church, or from professed Christians in the Church. However, that is when we need to call on CHRIST JESUS, WHO is the MASTER of the True Church.

If we take anything away from this passage, let it be this. Even though, the professed Church, as a whole, may sometimes disappoint us, or maybe the professed Pastor of the professed Church may even disappoint us. But, through it all, remember, we can always turn to CHRIST JESUS, because HE, will never disappoint us, and HE holds the key to joy and eternal life in HIS hands. And we can only achieve that kind of joy, and eternal life, through a show of "Honest, Saving Faith" in HIM, not, in our fellowman.

## PERSONAL APPLICATION:

(1). Remember that oftentimes unbelievers like to focus attention on the failures and shortcomings of Christians, and use them to try and discredit the name of JESUS, and the cause of Christianity. But people who are sincerely searching for the truth will eventually arrive at CHRIST, and, come to know that HIS power and authority is real.

(2). Don't become so disappointed with the servants of CHRIST that you abandon your search for the SAVIOR HIMSELF.

(3). Work hard to keep your focus on CHRIST and not the church, or those who claim to be servants of CHRIST, that way, you will never be disappointed that you chose to be a part of the body of CHRIST.

## LIFE RESPONSE:

Pray a prayer of thanks to GOD for sending us JESUS, WHO loves us so much, that HE stays faithful to us, even when we doubt HIM, and, that HE will help us to overcome our unbelief.

## KEY VERSE: Mark 9:24

## DEVOTIONAL PASSAGES: John 6:47-51, John 16:25-33, John 17:20-24

## LESSON THIRTEEN:

(44)


## THE INSTITUTION OF MARRIAGE
### (For better or for worse)


### SCRIPTURE:
The King James Version
(Mark 10:1-12)

**10** (1) And HE rose from thence, and cometh into the coasts of Judaea by the farther side of Jordan: and the people resort unto HIM again; and, as HE was wont, HE taught them again. (2) And the Pharisees came to HIM, and asked HIM, "Is it lawful for a man to put away his wife?" tempting HIM. (3) And HE answered and said unto them, "What did Moses command you?" (4) And they said, "Moses suffered to write a bill of divorcement, and to put her away." (5) And JESUS answered and said unto them, "For the hardness of your heart he wrote you this precept. (6) But from the beginning of the creation GOD made them male and female. (7) For this cause shall a man leave his father and mother, and cleave to his wife; (8) And they twain shall be one flesh: so then they are no more twain, but one flesh. (9) What therefore GOD hath joined together, let no man put asunder." (10) And in the house HIS disciples asked HIM again of the same matter. (11) And HE saith unto them, "Whosoever shall put away his wife, and marry another, committeth adultery against her. (12) And if a woman shall put away her husband, and be married to another, she committeth adultery."


### COMMENTARY:

As JESUS and HIS disciples left Galilee heading south toward Judea, and ultimately, to HIS final stop and appointment with death in Jerusalem, HE is met by a group of Pharisees who sought to tempt HIM with this question regarding the subject of divorce, "Is it lawful for a man to divorce his wife?"

Since here it says that the Pharisees sought to "tempt JESUS", it may have very well been that they were seeking to get HIM to contradict HIMSELF from what HE had stated earlier in HIS "Sermon on the Mount" regarding divorce (Matthew 5:31-32). Maybe they hoped, perhaps, that JESUS would give a self-incriminating answer that would help them to be able to mount some sort of opposition against HIM.

The Pharisees, and most Jewish men at that time, believed that a man could not commit adultery against his wife, and that, only the woman could be guilty of such an offense. They also held out hope that JESUS would take sides on this issue, or maybe they could cause a degree of dissention among JESUS' followers, that might divide them doctrinally.

But, whatever their underlying motives were, they were, once again, about to be disappointed, because JESUS counters their question, with a question of HIS own. In this passage HE asks them, "What did Moses say about divorce?" JESUS evidently was taking this opportunity to clear up their misunderstanding of this ancient Mosaic Law regarding divorce in Deuteronomy 24:1-4.

In Deuteronomy 24:1, GOD explains the only biblically allowable reason for a man to divorce his wife. Here HE says that the woman would have to have committed "undisclosed fornication" (ervah in the Hebrew) at some time prior to their marriage. In other words, she would have to have had pre-marrital sex with another man, and then later, not disclose it to the man she intends to marry. However, if she does disclose it to him before they are married, and then, he decides to marry her anyway, he cannot later use it as a reason to divorce her, but rather, he must remain married to her always, for GOD hates divorce, period (Malachi 2:16).

Here in this passage of Mark, JESUS explains, that, while divorce may be lawful in cases of undisclosed "pre-marrital sex" ("porneia" in the Greek), it is not permitted for cases of "adultery" ("Moicheia" in the Greek), which is sex with another person, outside of marriage.

JESUS had already explained this to the religious leaders in HIS, now famous "Sermon on the Mount", but just like most of us today, we still don't get it, simply because "we SO want to do what we want to do". However, we need to know that, within our sinful nature there is housed, "a lying spirit" that sometimes blocks us from accepting the "things of GOD, and until we release that spirit from our life, we won't ever come to grips completely with the finer points of GOD's Word.

In Matthew chapter 5, in JESUS' teachings about divorce, in verses 31-32, HE clearly explains GOD's position and law regarding this topic. There HE first gives them the misconceived or misunderstood version of "what man would like for the law of GOD to mean". Then, HE carefully explains to them what GOD truly says regarding divorce. What followed was perfectly in line with the concept of Deuteronomy 24:1.

JESUS, WHO is the Word in the flesh (John 1:1), says that, "You have heard that the Law of Moses says, "A man can divorce his wife by merely giving her a letter of divorce". Now, since JESUS really is the WORD in the flesh, coming from HIM, this is what HE may as well have been saying, "You have heard that "I said", a man can divorce his wife by merely giving her a letter of divorce, and that is not true".

Then, in verse 32, JESUS rebukes that notion and even denies that HE ever made such an ungodly statement that was now accredited to HIM. There HE says that, "A man who divorces his wife, except she commit fornication (porneia), which can only be committed by an unmarried person, who has no need of divorce, causes her to commit adultery (moicheia) (sex outside of marriage) by sending her away.

This tells us plainly that GOD doesn't release us from our marriage vows because of adultery, but only for undisclosed fornication. If we divorce a spouse because of adultery, as far as GOD is concerned, the two are still married and are committing adultery with the next person that they engage in sexual intercourse with.

Divorce, in GOD's eyes, only serves to show how far we've fallen short of the glorious standard that HE originally set for the institution of marriage. And therefore, in GOD's eyes, divorce is always sin, except for undisclosed fornication.

JESUS goes on to explain further to HIS disciples, after they had returned to the house where they were staying, that, "Any man, who divorces his wife, and remarries, commits adultery against the wife whom he sent away, and any woman, who divorces her husband, and remarries, commits adultery against the man whom she leaves" (Mark 10:10-12).

PERSONAL APPLICATION:

(1). The personal application here is crystal clear; GOD does not honor, nor does HE condone divorce, period.

(2). In a marriage, where either, or both spouses are Christian, the Christian, by way of their faith, pledges before GOD to abstain from adultery and fornication. and, even if only one spouse is a believer, that marriage is joined, in spiritual union with CHRIST, because, of the believer in the marriage. In other words, the husband, the wife, and CHRIST, become one in spirit and the marriage is sanctioned by GOD.

(3). There is always a spiritual link involved in sexual intercourse, which was intended by GOD, to first be used to consummate a marriage, and then to produce a family of offsprings from that marriage. When a man and a woman engage in sexual intercourse, during coition, the two involved, are spiritually fused into one spirit, whether they are married or not. Every time you have sex with a new person, you join yourself to their spirit. The number of sexual partners you've had, is the number of spirits you've joined yourself to, and carry around with you, as a part of your body! Our bodies were not made for sexual immorality (1 Corinthians 6:9-20).

## LIFE RESPONSE:

Pray to GOD for help with keeping your marriage in tact. Pray that HE remove from you, all those things that have caused you to consider divorcing your spouse, especially if the cause of those thoughts stem from sexual immorality. Pray that HE give you the most, clear understanding, of how sin is always at the root of divorce, and how we drag CHRIST into our sin with us, because HE too, is a part our marriage. Ask HIM for forgiveness, as well as, for the ability, to make your marriage right and pleasing to HIM, the way HE originally planned it, and that HE, give you the courage, and, strength in CHRIST, to keep it that way.

## KEY VERSE: Mark 10:7

## DEVOTIONAL PASSAGES: Genesis 2:20-24, 1Corinthians 7, Ephesians 5:21-33

# LESSON FOURTEEN:

(48)


## THE DANGERS OF PROSPERITY
### (How bad do we want Salvation?)


### SCRIPTURE:
The King James Version
(Mark 10:17-31)


**10** (17) And when HE was gone forth into the way, there came one running, and kneeled to HIM, and asked HIM, "Good MASTER, what shall I do that I may inherit eternal life?" (18) And JESUS said to him, "Why callest thou ME good? there is none good but one, that is, GOD. (19) thou knowest the commandments, Do not commit adultery, Do not kill, Do not steal, Do not bear false witness, Defraud not, Honour thy father and mother." (20) And he answered and said unto HIM, MASTER, all these have I observed from my youth." (21) Then JESUS beholding him loved him, and said unto him, "One thing thou lackest: go thy way, sell whatsoever thou hast, and give to the poor, and thou shalt have treasure in Heaven: and come, take up the cross, and follow ME." (22) And he was sad at that saying, and went away grieved: for he had great possessions. (23) And JESUS looked round about, and saith unto HIS disciples, "How hardly shall they that have riches enter into the kingdom of GOD!" (24) And the disciples were astonished at HIS words. But JESUS answereth again, and saith unto them, "Children, how hard is it for them that trust in riches to enter into the kingdom of GOD! (25) It is easier for a camel to go through the eye of a needle, than for a rich man to enter into the kingdom of GOD." (26) And they were astonished out of measure, saying among themselves, "Who then can be saved?" (27) And JESUS looking upon them saith, "With men it is impossible, but not with GOD: for with GOD all things are possible." (28) Then Peter began to say unto HIM, "Lo, we have left all, and have followed THEE." (29) And JESUS answered and said, "Verily I say unto you, There is no man who hath left house, or brethren, or sisters, or father, or mother, or wife, or children, or lands, for MY sake, and the Gospel's, (30) But he shall receive an hundredfold now in this time, houses, and brethren, and sisters, and mothers, and children, and lands, with persecutions; and in the world to come eternal life. (31) But many that are first shall be last; and the last first."

## COMMENTARY:

No one ever recognized the perils of prosperity, and the desire for material things as clearly as JESUS did. Material things are what attach a person's heart to this world. The more they gain, the more interest they have in it, and the more difficult they find it to ever, even momentarily think about leaving it.

It is said, that, out of a hundred people that can stand "adversity", only one of that hundred can stand "prosperity". A person is judged by two standards when it comes to prosperity; one, is how they came about it, and the other, is how they choose to use it. Will they use it as if they have undisputed possession of it? Or, will they remember that they hold it in stewardship to GOD?

With that being said, the question of this life ultimately becomes, "How bad do we want Salvation?" Do we want it bad enough to relinquish the people and things of this world? The rich young ruler here in Mark chapter 10, verses 17-31, as well as many of us, answer that question, in effect, "I want it, but I don't think I want it as much as all that".

It's all about Salvation, and here JESUS sums up the whole doctrine of Salvation in a nutshell, when he says, in effect, that, if a person is to depend upon their own efforts, to achieve salvation, then, it is impossible for anyone. Salvation is a gift from GOD, and with GOD, all things are possible. If a person relies on their own efforts, possessions, or riches, they can never enter into Salvation. However, if they rely upon the life giving power, and redeeming, agape love of CHRIST JESUS, they can enter, for free, into the kingdom of Heaven.

That's the very thought that JESUS sought to provoke here in this passage, and that's the very same thought that Paul, John, and all the New Testament writers wrote about, in all of their biblical literary efforts. And that thought still lingers in the minds of mature Christians, even today, because it goes to the very core, of the ideology of the Christian Faith.

The disciples were astounded when they heard JESUS' statement regarding the chances of a rich person making it into the kingdom of Heaven. In those days, and even now, a lot of people associate riches as being a sign of how blessed a person is, and, that that person must be walking closer with GOD, especially those rich individuals who are also heavy church goers. However, JESUS sought to put an end to that kind of foolish thinking that day, as they had stopped briefly, just east of the Jordan River, while HE was making the long trip back to Jerusalem for the final time.

Here JESUS makes it crystal clear that Salvation is not ours to earn, but rather, it is GOD's to give away, and we are more likely to accept that gift, if we don't lose our hearts, to the things of this world. A person's heart can only be given to GOD when they manage to tear it away from this world. And unless we give our hearts to GOD, we can never accept HIS gift of Salvation. We must come to the end of ourselves where JESUS is standing and waiting. Isn't it funny how that works? "We have to "give" to "receive". What a divine concept that is. And guess WHO thought of it. GOD!

## PERSONAL APPLICATION:

(1). Think about what some of your limits to following CHRIST might be. It might be a person, place, of thing.
(2). Which of those are you willing to give up for CHRIST JESUS?
(3). CHRIST gave up everything for us, and that's the example that HE expects us to follow.

## LIFE RESPONSE:

Pray to GOD for forgiveness for not putting HIM first, and then thank HIM for being faithful to you any way. Ask for the courage and strength that, HE already knows it takes, for us mere humans, to have the total faith in HIM that HE demands. Ask also that HE help you to suffer for that faith, until you can firmly believe that you really do hold it in your heart.

## KEY VERSES: Mark 10:26-27

## DEVOTIONAL PASSAGES: Matthew 6:19-34, Psalm 49:6-20, 2 Corinthians 8

LESSON FIFTEEN:

FAITH AND SIGHT
(What do you want from JESUS?)

SCRIPTURE:
The King James Version
(Mark 10:35-52)

**10** **35)** And James and John, the sons of Zebedee, come unto HIM, saying, "MASTER, we would that THOU shouldest do for us whatsoever we shall desire." **(36)** And HE said unto them, "What would ye that I should do for you?" **(37)** They said unto HIM, "Grant unto us that we may sit, one on THY right hand, and the other on THY left hand, in THY glory." **(38)** But JESUS said unto them, "Ye know not what ye ask: can ye drink of the cup that I drink of? and be baptized with the baptism that I am baptized with?" **(39)** And they said unto HIM, "We can". And JESUS said unto them, "Ye shall indeed drink of the cup that I drink of; and with the baptism that I am baptized withal shall ye be baptized: **(40)** But to sit on MY right hand and on MY left hand is not mine to give; but it shall be given to them for whom it is prepared." **(41)** And when the ten heard it, they began to be much displeased with James and John. **(42)** But JESUS called them to HIM, and saith unto them, "Ye know that they which are accounted to rule over the Gentiles exercise lordship over them; and their great ones exercise authority upon them. **(43)** But so shall it be among you: but whosoever will be great among you, shall be your minister: **(44)** And whosoever of you will be the chiefest, shall be servant of all. **(45)** For even the SON OF MAN came not to be ministered unto, but to minister, and to give HIS life a ransom for many."

**(46)** And they came to Jericho: and as HE went out of Jericho with HIS disciples and a great number of people, blind Bartimaeus, the son of Timaeus, sat by the highway side begging. **(47)** And when he heard that it was JESUS of Nazareth, he began to cry out, and say, "JESUS, THOU SON of David, have mercy on me." **(48)** And many charged him that he should hold his peace: but he cried the more a great deal, "THOU SON of David, have mercy on me." **(49)** And JESUS stood still, and commanded him to be called. And they call the blind man, saying unto him, "Be of good comfort, rise; HE calleth thee." **(50)** And he, casting away his garment, rose, and came to JESUS. **(51)** And JESUS answered and said unto him, "What wilt thou that I should do unto thee? The blind man said unto HIM, "LORD, that I might receive my sight." **(52)** And JESUS said unto him, "Go thy way; thy faith hath made thee whole." And immediately he received his sight, and followed JESUS in the way.

## COMMENTARY:

In Mark chapter 10, verse 43, as expressed in the original Greek, the word John Mark uses for "servant" is "diakonos" (dee-ak-on-os), and it describes a person who serves in a menial capacity. In JESUS' response to the request by James and John that HE grant them places of honor in HIS coming Kingdom, JESUS says, in summation that, "Whoever wishes to become great among you, shall be your servant, and whoever wishes to be first among you, shall be slave to all".

Here, in Mark 10:35-45, John Mark exposes something very human about the Disciples, and after all, they were just ordinary men. However, it is with such men, that JESUS set out to change the world, and history proves out that HE clearly succeeded in doing so. This passage not only gives us a peek at James and John's ambitiousness, but it also shows us their selfishness and pride, two things that they must rid themselves of if they are to become successful fishers of men under GOD.

This passage shows us that James and John had, to this point, completely failed to understand JESUS' examples of servitude, even as they had dwelt in HIS midst for the past three years. However, one thing does stand out in this passage, and it is that, James and John, as confused as they were, still believed in the coming Kingdom of CHRIST, and their hearts were still in the right place.

This story also tells us a lot about JESUS' standard of what greatness is. In verse 38, JESUS uses two well-known metaphors. First, HE asks, "Are you able to drink the cup that I drink?" And then HE asks, "Are you able to be baptized with the baptism, with which I am baptized with?" "Drink the cup", is the Jewish expression that means, "sharing one's fate or destiny". The "cup" is a symbol of both "joy" and "suffering". In the Old Testament, it often symbolized GOD's wrath against sin.

The term "baptism", here, symbolizes "someone deeply immersed in pain and troubles". Ultimately, both James and John did however, "drink the cup" and were "baptized with the baptism" of CHRIST. Acts 12:2 tells us that James became the first Disciple to be martyred, as he was killed with the sword at the ordering of King Herod Agrippa I.

And as for John, he lived a long life of persecution and suffering before, and after being exiled to the Greek island of Patmos by the Roman Emperor Domitian, where he later received a vision from GOD, and wrote the book of Revelations.

In the Greek, the word used for "ransom" is "lutron", and it describes "something that is used to "set free", something else. It also means "the cost, or price to redeem". The use of this word in verse 45, perhaps, makes it the key verse in John Mark's whole gospel account, because it clearly states the reason for which JESUS came into the World, and that is, "to redeem us".

The book of Mark was written to "make men see", through JESUS' miracles, that HE truly is the SON of the living GOD. In John 9:41, in JESUS' response to the Pharisee's question, "Are we blind also?" JESUS tells them that, "If you were blind, you wouldn't be guilty. But you remain guilty, because you claim you can see".

It is appropriate that we end this lesson with the story of blind Bartimaeus, who is depicted in Mark 10:46-52. Here, we see that this final miracle from JESUS is performed to "restore sight to the blind". However, the symbolism here speaks of spiritual blindness. And so it is also, with this literary effort, by John Mark, it is written to impart "spiritual insight" to the reader who may be "spiritually blind".

And as for JESUS, the end of the road was not far away. Jericho was only 15 miles from Jerusalem and HIS appointment with death on the cross. As JESUS passed by, they tried to silence a blind Bartimaeus, but he refused to let anyone take from him, his last chance to escape a world of darkness. When JESUS called for Bartimaeus, he immediately rose to his feet and went to HIM. He was determined to come out the darkness and into the light, and he knew that, only JESUS could provide him with such a gift.

The right time to come to JESUS is always "right now", and the right way to come to JESUS is always "just as you are". We don't have to fully understand JESUS before we come to HIM, for that, is something that we can never do. JESUS' demand is that we, have faith in GOD, and that is something that we can all do.

We don't have to become Theologians, before we become Christians, because Christianity is nothing more than a personal reaction to JESUS CHRIST. Bartimaeus' cure made him a by-product, of the good, that is in CHRIST

JESUS. And after he received his miracle from JESUS, he did not go selfishly on his way. Showing his gratitude, he followed JESUS, because that's what true Discipleship is all about.

## PERSONAL APPLICATION:

(1). James and John wanted to sit next to JESUS in Heaven. Bartimaeus wanted JESUS to restore his sight. What do you want JESUS to do for you?

(2). Sometimes we can be so focused on our desired answer to our prayers from GOD, that we actually miss the answer that HE gives us. GOD wants us to desire the things that HE already knows are best for us. HE will not give us something that HE knows will not serve as a blessing to us and others. Anything that does you harm, GOD will not grant, because, if HE did, it wouldn't be a blessing.

(3). Next time, before you pray and ask anything of GOD, consider what is important to GOD, and what falls in line with HIS will for your life according to Scripture. Many things that we ask for are not even within HIS will, and then, some things that we ask for may not be good for us as individuals, and also, some things we pray for may not be good for us in the present, but GOD, through HIS wisdom will know when the time is right for us to receive it in the future.

(4). GOD wants us to have everything our heart desires, but HE will never give us anything that will harm us, or cause us to harm anyone else in any way. We must learn to pray in the power of the HOLY SPIRIT.

## LIFE RESPONSE:

Pray and ask GOD to teach you how to pray for those things that JESUS wants for you, because those things are always the ones that are best for you. And then, thank HIM that we have JESUS to turn to for all of our desires that are also good for us, and all of our daily needs, period.

**KEY VERSE: Mark 10:45**


**DEVOTIONAL PASSAGES: John 20:24-31, Matthew 6:25-34, Matthew 7:7-11**

# LESSON SIXTEEN:

## JESUS' TRIUMPHANT ENTRY INTO JERUSALEM
### (JESUS demands respect and worship)

### SCRIPTURE:
The King James Version
(Mark 11:1-18)

**11** (1) And when they came nigh to Jerusalem, unto Bethphage and Bethany, at the mount of Olives, HE sendeth forth two of HIS disciples, (2) And saith unto them, "Go your way unto the village over against you; and as soon as ye be entered into it, ye shall find a colt tied, whereon never man sat; loose him, and bring him, (3) And if any man say unto you, Why do ye this? say ye that the LORD hath need of HIM; and straightway he will send him hither." (4) And they went their way, and found the colt tied by the door without in a place where two ways met; and they loose him. (5) And certain of them that stood there said unto them, "What do ye, loosing the colt?" (6) And they said unto them even as JESUS had commanded: and they let them go. (7) And they brought the colt to JESUS, and cast their garments on him; and HE sat upon him. (8) And many spread their garments in the way: and others cut down branches off the trees, and strawed them in the way. (9) And they that went before, and they that followed, cried, saying, "Hosanna; blessed is HE that cometh in the name of the LORD: (10) Blessed be the kingdom of our father David, that cometh in the name of the LORD: Hosanna in the highest." (11) And JESUS entered into Jerusalem, and into the temple: and when HE had looked round about upon all things, and now the eventide was come, HE went out unto Bethany with the twelve. (12) And on the morrow, when they were come from Bethany, HE was hungry: (13) And seeing a fig tree afar off having leaves, HE came, if haply HE might find any thing thereon: and when HE came to it, HE found nothing but leaves; for the time of figs was not yet. (14) And JESUS answered and said unto it, "No man eat fruit of thee hereafter for ever." And HIS disciples heard it. (15) And they come to Jerusalem: and JESUS went into the temple, and began to cast out them that sold and bought in the temple, and overthrew the tables of the moneychangers, and the seats of them that sold doves; (16) And would not suffer that any man should carry any vessel through the temple. (17) And HE taught, saying unto them, "Is it not written, MY house shall be called of all nations the house of prayer? but ye have made it a den of thieves." (18) And the scribes and chief priests heard it, and sought how they might destroy HIM: for they feared HIM, because all the people was astonished at HIS doctrine.

## COMMENTARY:

Mark chapter 11 marks the beginning of the last week of JESUS' physical life here on Earth. John Mark opens the chapter with a vivid description of JESUS, setting the stage for HIS triumphant entry into Jerusalem. It is the last leg of JESUS' incredible journey in route to HIS own execution.

When JESUS rode into Jerusalem that day, HE claimed to be a King. But, by riding in on a Donkey, HE was claiming to be a King of peace. Here in this passage we see the peoples' treating of JESUS' arrival at Jerusalem, as if it were a long-awaited, physical conquest. It is even suggested in their shouts of "Hosanna" in verse 9, which means "save us now".

Their welcome of JESUS was one that befitted a Conqueror, who was there to slay the enemy of HIS people. However, they didn't realize that their real enemy was always satan, and he had long held them captive in their own sin. And so, in that sense JESUS really had conquered their enemy, and HE was doing so by overcoming satan and all of the temporal things he has to offer to the world.

When JESUS arrived in Jerusalem late one afternoon, HE went into the temple and looked around very carefully, probably seeing that it was all set up with the merchant's booth, where they would open up for business the following day to sell Passover sacrifice items to the people. However, HE took no action that day because it was very late and no one was inside.

The following day, however, after HE had returned from Bethany with HIS disciples, JESUS went directly to the Temple and begin to cast out the unsavory characters that were found within. In the biblical Greek, the word used to describe "GOD's goodness in discipline" is "agathosune" ( ag-ath-o-soo-nay). It is a word that does not occur in secular Greek. This is the word that applies to JESUS' actions in verses 15-17, when HE ejected the robbers and moneychangers from the temple because they had desecrated GOD's Holy Place.

By overcharging the people for animals, used to give as sacrifices to GOD at the Temple, and, also by charging them too large of a fee to convert their money over to the proper local currency, the merchants were, in effect, blocking the poorest people, and Gentiles, who were not allowed beyond the outer court of the temple, from worshipping GOD.

Here, JESUS seeks to remind us to be very careful not to block anyone from worshipping GOD, because of their social, racial, or economic differences and pedigree, nor, through our selfishness and greed. GOD, loves not just the Jews, but desires all the nations of the world, be they rich, or poor, Jew or Gentile, to be saved.

There is, perhaps, no other place in Scriptures, where we feel reminded, that we need to make a more conscious effort to be fair in our dealings with each other. There were many crooked people in the Temple Court that day, but there were also many others, whose hearts were set on GOD. The LORD will never hold blameless, those who make it hard, or impossible for others to worship HIM.

Sometimes, even ministers of GOD, can be more concerned, with imposing their ways of doing things on their congregation, than they are, with preaching and teaching the Word of GOD. Remember, JESUS didn't send everyone in the temple away that day, but rather, it only those who were blocking the worship of GOD, by making it difficult, or impossible for the poorest among them to afford animal sacrifices used in worship of HIM.


## PERSONAL APPLICATION:

(1). Do you worship GOD only once a week, and continue to not give HIM the respect HE deserves, during all the other days? Do you even worship HIM once a week?

(2). You can begin to understand the importance of giving respect and honor to CHRIST, by enlightening your mind to the facts of the "Most High Faith". As you come to know CHRIST more, the more your heart will warm to HIM, and you will began to worship and praise HIM for all that HE is doing, has done, and will do in your life.

(3). JESUS' victorious entry into Jerusalem, and, HIS subsequent cleansing of the temple, are symbolic of what HE wants to do in each of our hearts, but remember, HE must be invited in (Revelation 3:20). HE will not force HIS way into your life.

## LIFE RESPONSE:

Pray and invite JESUS to come into your life, and overturn and remove, all those things in your life that are contrary to the will of GOD, and, that grieve the HOLY SPIRIT.

### KEY VERSE: Mark 11:15

### DEVOTIONAL PASSAGES: Zechariah 9:9-12, Matthew 21:1-16, Psalm 8:1-2

# LESSON SEVENTEEN:

## THE MOST IMPORTANT COMMANDMENT
### (The love for GOD and the Love for our fellowman)

### SCRIPTURE:
### The King James Version
### (Mark 12:28-34)

**12** **(28)** And one of the scribes came, and having heard them reasoning together, and perceiving that HE had answered them well, asked HIM, "Which is the first commandment of all?" **(29)** And JESUS answered him, "The first of all the commandments is, Hear O Israel; The LORD our GOD is one LORD: **(30)** And thou shalt love the LORD thy GOD with all thy heart, and with all thy soul, and with all thy mind, and with all thy strength: this is the first commandment. **(31)** And the second is like, namely this, thou shalt love thy neighbor as thyself. There is none other commandment greater than these." **(32)** And the scribe said unto HIM, "Well, MASTER, THOU hast said the truth: for there is one GOD; and there is none other but HE:" **(33)** And to love HIM with all the heart, and with all the understanding, and with all the soul, and with all the strength, and to love his neighbour as himself, is more than all whole burnt offerings and sacrifices." **(34)** And when JESUS saw that he answered discreetly, HE said unto him, "Thou art not far from the kingdom of GOD." And no man after that durst ask HIM any question.

## COMMENTARY:

In Mark chapter 12, verses 28-34, one of the teachers of religious law, probably a Pharisee, was standing close by, listening to JESUS' answer to the Sadducees, regarding the resurrection. The Sadducees were a group of wealthy Jewish men who prided themselves as being experts in the knowledge of religious law. They also did not believe there would be a resurrection of life after death.

This particular teacher, who apparently had more insight than the others, and perceiving how well JESUS had answered the Sadducees question, poses this question of his own to JESUS, "Which is the first commandment of all? Here, the Greek word translated "which" is "poios", which means "what kind of", and the Greek word translated "first" "protos", means "most important". And so, here, JESUS is being asked, in effect, "Which is the most important commandment?

JESUS begins by reciting the opening line, of the first part of the three-part "Shema", which was recited by devout Jews twice daily. It stresses the unity of GOD, and, the importance of loving HIM and HIS Laws, and it goes like this; "Hear old Israel; the LORD our GOD is one LORD" (Deuteronomy 6:4).

To love the LORD THY GOD with all thy heart, soul, mind, and strength calls for a thorough commitment to GOD that is both personal, and whole of heart. It speaks to the entire human personally; the heart, which is the center of human life, the soul, which is the "self-conscience" life of all men, the mind, which is the entire thought process of man and, of course, the strength, or entire physical power of man.

In other words, we should "love GOD with every fiber of our being". This is what is covered in the first four commandments (see Exodus 20:3-11), where it tells us, in effect, that our love for GOD must be totally loyal (verse 3), totally faithful (verse 6), totally trusting (verse 7), and show total reverence (verse 8).

Next, JESUS states that we should love our neighbor as we love ourselves. This is the concept of the remaining six commandments (Exodus 20:12-17). If we love each other, we can certainly begin with honoring our own parents. If we love each other, we are not likely to intentionally, or maliciously take another's life, which by the way, is made in the "spiritual image" of GOD.

Also, if we love each other, we will not commit adultery against our spouse with another person. If we love each other, we won't steal from each other. If we love each other, we won't lie on each other, or falsely accuse each other. And finally, if we love each other, we won't jealously desire anything that belongs to someone else. And so I guess, in summation, JESUS is saying that, everything, that GOD commands us to do, is of the utmost importance to HIM.


PERSONAL APPLICATION:

(1). Through HIS Holy Word, learn to love GOD, with all your Heart, Soul, Mind, and physical strength. Go ahead! Open up your bible, and get started right now.
(2). Through GOD's word we can learn to love our neighbor, as much as we love ourselves. Go ahead! Open up your door, and get started right away.
(3). Once you get started, you won't be far from the kingdom of Heaven.

LIFE RESPONSE:

Pray to GOD and ask that HE permeate your heart, soul, mind, and spirit with love for HIM, and, for your fellowman. Ask that HE also give you the strength to be able to pass that spirit of love on to someone else, each and every day, for the remainder of your life here on earth.

KEY VERSES: Mark 12:30-31

DEVOTIONAL PASSAGES: Exodus 20:3-17

# LESSON EIGHTEEN:

### A NEW MEANING FOR PASSOVER
(JESUS willingly sacrificed HIS body and blood for us)

### SCRIPTURE:
The King James Version
(Mark 14:12-26)

**14** (12) And the first day of unleavened bread, when they killed the Passover, HIS disciples said unto HIM, "Where wilt THOU that we go and prepare that THOU mayest eat the Passover?" (13) And HE sendeth forth two of HIS disciples, and saith unto them, "Go ye into the city, and there shall meet you a man bearing a pitcher of water: follow him. (14) And wheresoever he shall go in, say ye to the goodman of the house, THE MASTER saith, Where is the questchamber, Where I shall eat the Passover with MY disciples?" (15) And he will show you a large upper room furnished and prepared: there make ready for us. (16) And HIS disciples went forth, and came into the city, and found as HE had said unto them: and they made ready the Passover. (17) And in the evening HE cometh with the twelve. (18) And as they sat and did eat, JESUS said, "Verily I say unto you, one of you which eateth with ME shall betray ME" (19) And they began to be sorrowful, and to say unto HIM one by one, "is it I?" and another said, "is it I?" (20) And HE answered and said unto them, "It is one of the twelve, that dippeth with ME in the dish. (21) The SON OF MAN indeed goeth, as it is written of HIM: but woe to that man by whom the SON OF MAN is betrayed! Good were it for that man if he had never been born. (22) And as they did eat, JESUS took bread, and blessed, and brake it, and gave to them, and said, "Take, eat: this is MY body." (23) And HE took the cup, and when HE had given thanks, HE gave it to them: and they all drank of it. (24) And HE said unto them, "This is MY blood of the new testament, which is shed for many. (25) Verily I say unto you, I will drink no more of the fruit of the vine, until that day that I drink it new in the kingdom of GOD." (26) And when they had sung an hymn, they went out into the mount of Olives.

### PREPARING FOR THE FEAST: A LOOK AT COMMUNION SERVICE

Scripture shows us again and again how efficient JESUS was in planning and arrangement. We see over and over again how HE did not leave things unprepared until the last moment. All of HIS arrangements were made far in advance.

In Matthew's account of the last week of JESUS' life, in chapter 26, starting at verse 17 (KJV), we see HIS Disciples coming to HIM inquiring, where HE wanted them to prepare the Passover Feast? JESUS sent them into Jerusalem with instructions to look for a man and tell him that, "MY time is at hand; I will keep the Passover at thy house with MY Disciples".

However in John Mark's Gospel account, in chapter 14, verses 13-15 (KJV), we pick up a few more details. We see JESUS instructing them to look for a man carrying a pitcher of water. This sort of instruction is an obvious pre-arranged signal, because in those days, carrying pots of water was strictly a woman's duty. To see a man performing this chore would be extremely unusual, and would be a sure-fire way of identifying the right man.

Now, let's examine why this man's house would be a good place for JESUS and HIS disciple's Passover Supper. In those days, the larger Jewish houses had upper rooms. They were constructed in such a manner, that they resembled a smaller box that was stacked on top of a larger box. The smaller "upper room", which could be accessed by way of an outside stairway, served multiple purposes. It was used as a storage area, quest room, or just a quiet place of meditation. But customarily, it was used as a place where Jewish Rabbis would come to teach. This particular man had just such a house.

According to the way the Jews count days, the new day begins at 6:00 o'clock in the evening. The Passover day, itself, is on the 14th Nisan, but preparation for Passover is done on the 13th Nisan, and is completed by 6:00 p.m. In preparing for Passover, there is first, a "ceremonial search for leaven". Every bit of "leaven" must be totally removed from a household. This is in conformance with the tradition of the very first Passover in Egypt, as it is recorded in Exodus 12, where it was commemorated with the eating of "unleavened bread".

Then, on the afternoon of the 13th Nisan, came the "sacrificing of the Passover Lamb". All the people would come to the temple and the worshippers would each kill their own lamb for sacrifice. Two long lines of priests stood between the worshippers and the Altar, each holding a gold or silver bowl. When the lamb's throat was slit, the blood was caught in one of these bowls, and was passed up the line to the priest at the end of the line, who would pour the blood onto the Altar.

The lamb is then skinned and gutted, and the fat is extracted. The meat is then handed back to the worshipper, and it is then, carried home to be roasted on an open fire with a spit made of Pomegranate wood. The table that is used is shaped like a square with one end open. It was very low, and the diners were reclined on couches, resting on their left arm, with their right arm free for eating.

**This is a list of things that were necessary for the Disciples to obtain for the Passover meal:**

(1). There is the "Lamb": It is to remind them of how their houses had been protected by the blood of the lamb when the Angel of Death passed through Egypt, on the eve, of the great exodus.

(2). There is the "Unleavened Bread": This is to remind them of the bread that they had eaten in haste, when they left out, from slavery in Egypt.

(3). There is the "Bowl of Salt Water": To remind them of the tears that they had shed in Egypt, and the water of the Red Sea, through which they had miraculously passed to safety.

(4). There is the collection of "Bitter Herbs": Horse Radish, Chicory, Endive, Lettuce, and Horehound to remind them of the bitterness of slavery in Egypt.

(5). There is a paste called "Charosheth" (Khar-o-sheth): A mixture of Apples, Dates, Pomegranates, and nuts, to remind them of the clay, of which they had to make bricks in Egypt. Also mixed through it, were sticks of cinnamon to remind them of the straw, with which the bricks had been made.

(6). There were the "Four Cups of Wine": The cups contained a little more than half a pint of wine, with three parts wine mixed with two parts water. The four cups were drank at different stages of the Passover meal, and were to remind them of the four promises in Exodus 6:6-7, where GOD says, "I will bring you out from under the burdens of the Egyptians". "I will rid you out of their bondage". "I will redeem you with a stretched out arm, and with great judgments". "I will take you to ME for a people, and I will be to you a GOD".

**Now this is the procedure, or various steps by which the Passover Meal is eaten:**

(1). First the "Cup of the Kiddush" (first of the four cups of wine) is prayed over and drank. "Kiddush" means "sanctification", or "separation". This cup symbolizes the separation of this meal from all other common meals. The head of the family prays over the cup, and then everyone would drink it.

(2).Then there is the "first hand washing", which would be done only by the person who was to celebrate the feast. They must wash their hands three times in a prescribed way.

(3). Now, a piece of parsley, or lettuce was taken and dipped in the bowl of salt water and eaten as an appetizer to the meal. The parsley, or lettuce symbolized the hyssop, with which the blood had been smeared over the doorposts in Egypt.

(4). "The breaking of the Bread". Two blessings are used in the breaking of the bread. "Blessed be THOU, O LORD, our God, King of the universe, who bringest forth from the earth", or "Blessed art THOU, our FATHER in Heaven, who givest us today the bread necessary for us". On the table, there are three circles of unleavened bread. The middle one is taken and broken, to remind them that as slaves, they never had a whole loaf to eat. As it is broken, the head of the family would say, "This is the bread of affliction that our forefathers ate in Egypt. Whosoever is hungry, let him come and eat. Whosoever is in need let him come and keep Passover with us".

(5). Next came the telling of the "Story of Deliverance", or, how GOD delivered the Jews out, of Egypt.

(6). Then Psalms 113 & 114 are sung. Psalms 113-118 are known as the "Hallel", which means "the praise of GOD".

(7). Then the second cup of wine is drunk. It is called the "Cup of Haggadah", which means "the cup of explaining or proclaiming".

(8). Afterwards, all those present, now wash their hands in preparation for the meal.

(9). A grace is said. "Blessed art THOU, O LORD, our God, who bringest forth fruit from the earth. Blessed art THOU, O GOD, who has sanctified us with THY commandment and enjoined us to eat unleavened cakes". Then small pieces of bread are distributed.

(10). Some of the bitter Herbs are placed between the two pieces of bread and are dipped in the Charosheth and then eaten. This is called "the Sop", and is what JESUS is referring to in the Gospels, when HE is identifying Judas Iscariot as the person who will betray HIM.

(11). Now comes the Meal Proper, or the eating of the Lamb. All the meat must be eaten, or the leftovers must be destroyed to assure that they are not used later in a common meal.

(12). The hands are again washed.

## The next two steps, are the one's, which JESUS made, HIS own, and, which we commemorate, during our (Baptist) Communion Services:

(13). The remainder of the unleavened bread is eaten.

(14). There is a prayer of Thanksgiving, containing a petition for the coming of Elijah, to herald the MESSIAH. Then the third cup is drank, which is called the "Cup of Thanksgiving". Then this blessing is said: "Blessed art THOU, O LORD, our God, King of the universe, who hast created the fruit of the vine".

(15). The second part of the Hallel, Psalms 115-118, is sung.
(16). The forth cup is drank, and Psalms 136, which is known as the "Great Hallel" is sung.
(17). Two short prayers are prayed to end the Passover Meal:

"All THY works shall praise THEE, O LORD, our God. And THY Saints, the righteous, who do THY good pleasure, and all thy people, the house of Israel, with joyous song, let them praise and bless and magnify and glorify and exalt and reverence and sanctify and scribe the Kingdom to THY name, O GOD, our King. For it is good to praise THEE, and pleasure to sing praises to THY name, from everlasting to everlasting THOU art GOD.

—

"The breath of all that lives shall praise THY name, O LORD, our God. And the spirit of all flesh shall continually glorify and exalt THY memorial, O GOD, our King. For from everlasting unto everlasting THOU art GOD, and besides THEE we have no King, Redeemer, or Savior".

The words "in remembrance", that JESUS uses in HIS instituting of the LORD's Supper, dates back to the Old Testament concept of "Zikkaron" (Zik-ka-rone). Zikkaron is a Festival, Practice, or Object, that is used to symbolically link future generations to a distinctive act of GOD. The name derives from the Hebrew word "zikrown" (zik-rone), which means "a memento, or memorable thing, day, or writing".

Through the Zikkaron, GOD's people could sense their personal participation, along with the original generation, in the act that GOD had performed for them. Thus the LORD's Supper is a unique institution of sacrament, intended to link all generations to the memory of CHRIST JESUS' vicarious sacrifice.

The New Covenant is mentioned many times in the Old Testament, and it is spelled out quite clearly by GOD, in Jeremiah 31:31-34. JESUS came to usher in that new Covenant from GOD. It is a Covenant that is far superior to any before, or since, that time. This New Covenant provides for the regeneration of mankind, and allots for us to be indwelt by the HOLY SPIRIT, when we come to believe in JESUS CHRIST. The bread, which we eat at the sacrament, is common bread, but for those who have the heart to feel and understand, it is the very body of CHRIST.

In the Gospel according to Luke, as expressed in 22:22, in his original Greek writings, the word Luke uses in JESUS' statement, that translates "determined", is "horizo" (hor-id-zo). Luke is the only author in Scripture who uses this particular translation for "determined", and he uses it only here, and in Acts 17:26. In both places it means "decreed by GOD", and is meant to remind us, from a "time-bound" perspective, that JESUS' death was a miscarriage of justice, and that, from GOD's point of view, it was the keystone of HIS plan to, not only provide salvation, but to also, set all things right.

In Exodus 24:1-8, the Israelites accepted GOD's Covenant, as it had been given to Moses on Mount Sinai. The continuance of that Covenant depended on man keeping his pledge and obeying the laws of GOD. But man could not then, and quite frankly, cannot now, abide by such a Covenant, because our sin continuously interrupts our relationship with GOD. It took the life of CHRIST to restore that lost relationship, of friendship with GOD. "This do in remembrance of me", is what JESUS said to HIS Disciples. But it is also a statement that comes to us, from across the spans of time, in hopes that we too, can share in HIS new Covenant.

JESUS knew how quickly the human mind would forget. HE knew that we would become so preoccupied with our own worldly affairs, that, eventually, we would fail to recall HIS vicarious sacrifice. And so, HE invites us to, come in sometimes, into the peace and tranquility, of HIS FATHER's House, and to "Do this in remembrance of HIM".

It is all the more tragic that, at that very table, on that Passover night, in a dimly lit upper room, somewhere in the midst, of the festive atmosphere of Jerusalem, that there sat one, who was a traitor, and, who would sell JESUS out, for the price of a common slave, which was thirty pieces of silver, at that time.

Since the birth of the New Covenant, at every Communion table, there are those who would betray JESUS. If, in HIS House, we pledge ourselves to HIM, and then, go out and fail to reflect HIS image to others, through our own behavior, then we too, like Judas, have become traitors to HIS cause.

Unlike JESUS, we don't know when our last supper will be. It is the will of GOD that man not know what his place, time, or method of demise will be. But, like JESUS, we can all, become great preparers, and begin to store up our treasures in a place that JESUS says, "has been prepared for us, from the foundation of this World". That place that Luke, Paul, and other New Testament writers call, in the Greek, "Paradeisos" (Par-ad-i-sos), but we call, "the Kingdom of Heaven".

## PERSONAL APPLICATION:

(1). During the final week of JESUS' life on earth, HE introduced us to, what we now call "The LORD's Supper", or "Communion". What arc some of the thoughts that go through your mind, during Communion services?

(2). Can you make a commitment to yourself to honor CHRIST's sacrifice in some way, during the coarse of each day, by way of prayer, good deed, etc.?

(3). If you never realized, before this lesson, what a marvelous sacrifice JESUS has made for you, and you now want to put your faith and trust in the LORD, pray a prayer of repentance and then ask the LORD how you can be a better steward with the life HE has given you, in honor of CHRIST JESUS.

## LIFE RESPONSE:

Pray a prayer of thanksgiving to the LORD for HIS wonderful sacrifice, and how, with open eyes, HE accepted the circumstances of the cross, so that, whosoever believes in HIM, will not perish, but rather, will have, life eternal in the kingdom of GOD.

## KEY VERSE: Mark 14:24

## DEVOTIONAL PASSAGES: 1 Corinthians 11:23-28, Matthew 26:17-30, Luke 22:7-30

# LESSON NINETEEN:

(70)

JESUS ON TRIAL
(We find no fault in HIM)

SCRIPTURE:
The King James Version
(Mark 14:53-65 & 15:1-15)

**14** (53) And they led JESUS away to the high priest: and with HIM were assembled all the high priests and the elders and the scribes. (54) And Peter followed HIM afar off, even into the palace of the high priest: and he sat with the servants, and warmed himself at the fire. (55) And the chief priests and all the council sought for witness against JESUS to put HIM to death; and found none. (56) For many bare false witness against HIM, but their witness agreed not together. (57) And there arose certain, and bare false witness against HIM, saying, (58) "We heard HIM say, I will destroy this temple that is made with hands, and within three days I will build another made without hands." (59) But neither so did their witness agree together. (60) And the high priest stood up in the midst, and asked JESUS, saying, "Answerest THOU nothing? What is it which these witness against THEE?" (61) But HE held HIS peace, and answered nothing. Again the high priest asked HIM, and said unto HIM, "Art THOU the CHRIST, the SON of the BLESSED? (62) And JESUS said, "I AM: and ye shall see the SON OF MAN sitting on the right hand of power, and coming in the clouds of Heaven." (63) Then the high priest rent his clothes, and saith, "What need we any further witness? (64) Ye have heard the blasphemy: what think ye? And they all condemned HIM to be guilty of death. (65) And some began to spit on HIM, and to cover HIS face, and to buffet HIM, and to say unto HIM, prophesy: and the servants did strike HIM with the palm of their hands.

**15** (1) And straightway in the morning the chief priests held a consultation with the elders and scribes and the whole council, and bound JESUS, and carried HIM away, and delivered HIM to Pilate. (2) And Pilate asked HIM, "Art THOU the KING of the Jews? And HE answering said unto him, "Thou sayest it." (3) And the chief priests accused HIM of many things: but HE answered nothing. (4) And Pilate asked HIM again, saying, "Answerest THOU nothing? Behold how many things they witness against THEE."

(5) But JESUS yet answered nothing; so that Pilate marveled. (6) Now at that feast he released unto them one prisoner, whomsoever they desired. (7) And there was one named Barabbas, which lay bound with them that had made insurrection with him, who had committed murder in the insurrection. (8) And the multitude crying aloud began to desire him to do as he had ever done unto them. (9) But Pilate answered them, saying, "Will ye that I release unto you the KING of the Jews?" (10) For he knew that the chief priests had delivered HIM for envy. (11) But the chief priests moved the people, that he should rather release Barabbas unto them. (12) And Pilate answered and said again unto them, "What will ye then that I shall do unto HIM WHOM ye call the KING of the Jews?" (13) And they cried out again, "Crucify HIM". (14) Then Pilate said unto them, "Why, what evil hath HE done? And they cried out the more exceedingly, "Crucify HIM". (15) And so Pilate, willing to content the people, released Barabbas unto them, and delivered JESUS, when HE had scourged HIM, to be crucified.

## COMMENTARY:

In Mark 14:53-65 and 15:1-15 John Mark gives us his account of the "Trials of CHRIST JESUS". There, we see JESUS, first standing trial before the "Sanhedrin", the group that was the religious authority of the day, and subsequently, we see HIM before the Roman Procurator of Judea, Pontius Pilate.

During the time of JESUS' trials, (six in all, when we combine the synoptic gospels Matthew, Mark, and Luke together), the powers of the Sanhedrin were limited. Even though they had full power over all religious matters, according to Jewish records, forty years before the destruction of the Temple at Jerusalem, judgment in matters of life and death had been taken away from the Jews by Caesar.

While it is true that sometimes, as, in the case of Stephen (Acts 7:54-60), where they stoned him to death, the Jews did take the law into their own hands. But legally, they had no right to apply the death penalty to anyone. And, that is why, they had to bring JESUS to Pilate, to be crucified (John 18:31).

The key word here is "Crucifixion", as the Sanhedren wasn't so concerned about observing Roman law, as the stoning of Stephen proves, however, in this case, they didn't just want to kill JESUS, but they also wanted to discredit HIM, and ensure that HE wouldn't become Martyred by HIS OWN death.

Crucifixion on a cross was the same as being hung from a tree. The Jews believed that anyone hung from a tree was "cursed of GOD". They based this belief on what is written in Deuteronomy 21:22-23. Therefore, in their minds, Crucifixion (death by Roman method) would prove, once and for all, that JESUS could not have been the Messiah, and in fact, HIS manner of death would stand as proof that HE was, quite literally, "cursed of GOD", and their own claims would be vindicated.

That is why Paul has to explain in his letter to the Galatians (Galatians 3:13-14) some time later, that, JESUS "rescued" us from the "curse" pronounced by the law. There he was referring the statement in Deuteronomy 21:22-23, and is attempting to separate JESUS' death on the cross from that context, and rightfully so. When JESUS was hung on the cross, HE took upon HIMSELF, the "curse" of our wrongdoing, and therefore the opposite occurred, and the curse became a blessing for all mankind.

Now let's take a moment to learn a little bit about Pontius Pilate, the man who sentenced JESUS, first to be scourged with lead tipped whips, and later to death by Crucifixion. What little information that is known about Pilate before that fateful day in A.D. 28, when he had his encounter with CHRIST, is provided by the Jewish historian Josephus Flavius, who, not only was a writer from close to that time period, but also was a General in the Galilean Army, during it's war against Rome (A.D. 66-70).

He tells us that Pilate was born a Roman citizen, into a wealthy family. He was appointed to his post as Procurator, in A.D. 26 by Tiberius, who was the second Emperor of Rome, and Caesar Augustus Octavian's successor. He was married to a woman named Claudia Procula, and, after his appointment, they came to live in Caesarea, the headquarters of the province of Judea.

Pilate governed the areas of Judea, Samaria, and also, the areas south to the Dead Sea and Gaza. He had absolute authority over all non-Roman citizens of his province. He never became popular with the Jews, because he was insensitive to their religious convictions, and stubborn in his pursuit of his own policies.

When he first came to Jerusalem, he angered the Jews by refusing to remove the image of the Roman Emperor, Tiberius from their helmets. Octavian, Tiberius, Claudius, and Nero, were all considered to be gods, during their reigns as Emperors. The images of these men represented idolatry to the Jews, and every governor before Pilate had respected the Jews religious beliefs, and removed this insignia from the front of their helmets.

Pilate also greatly angered the Jews, on another occasion, when he took money from the Temple treasury to build an Aqueduct system to supply water to

Jerusalem. Many Jews reacted violently to this act, and Pilate's soldiers killed many of them in a rebellion, that is referred to in Luke 13:1-2. If either one of these incidents had been reported to Rome, it could have cost Pilate his job, and maybe even his life.

The Romans had a strict policy against inciting civil disturbances. Many Scholars and Theologians believe that the Sanhedrin used these incidences, as leverage to blackmail Pilate into carrying out JESUS' death sentence for them. John hints at this possibility in chapter 19, verse 12, where he writes, "if you release this man you are not Caesar's friend".

And so we see here, the grim truth of a man's past catching up with him, and, if that be the case, then Pilate sacrificed justice, in order to keep his job. He sentenced JESUS to death, so that he might remain Governor of Palestine.

During these trials of JESUS, one can't help but notice, the many paradoxes that emerge;

- First of all, we see the religious leaders of GOD's people putting GOD THE SON on trial.
- Then we see a representative of an earthly king errantly condemn the KING of all Kings.
- Here we also see the people call for the freedom of a guilty man (Barabbas), and the death of an innocent man (JESUS), in his stead.
- And finally, we see the PRINCE OF PEACE dying a violent death.

And so Pilate's wavering, during JESUS' trial, should not be mistaken for virtue. For, a quick look at his personal history shows us that he ultimately chose the path of least resistance, in order to save himself, from his own, self-imposed, troubled career. However, he should have known that the truth can never be compromised. We either hold fast to the things of GOD, or we allow ourselves to be deceived by satan.

The Jewish leaders delivered JESUS into the hands of Pilate, and he tried to compromise. He even, on the surface, convinced himself that he had done all that he could, but actually he knew, even deeper in his heart, that he had long ago, tossed away the option to do the right thing. He had unwittingly set himself up for blackmail by the Jewish hierarchy, and they now saw this as an opportune time to call it in.

The permissive will of GOD allows for man to do many things, and ultimately, through JESUS' death, we also receive, in addition, GOD's wonderful and abounding Grace. However, GOD, through his wisdom, will never allow grace to "trump" TRUTH. The TRUTH presented itself to Pilate that day, in the person of JESUS CHRIST, and he decided to put TRUTH to death.

And, as for the Jews, in order to carry out the death of JESUS, they abandoned every principal they ever had, especially, that day, when they uttered those infamous words to Pilate, as it is recorded in John 19:15, where they declare, "We have no King but Caesar".

That put the final "brush strokes" on a "tragic painting", of a maddened mob that had been driven by anger. Driven by their hatred for JESUS, the Jews lost all sense of proportion, and they totally forgot about the mercy they had so often preached about in the Temple. They forgot all about justice, and in the end, denounced GOD, and professed Caesar.

Never before in the history of man has hatred's insanity presented itself to us more vividly, and hopefully, it never will again. There can never be a right time to do the wrong thing, as Pilate and the Jews ultimately did. In their case, they took the most beautiful LIGHT that ever did live, and then, they snuffed HIM out, on a cross.

## PERSONAL APPLICATION:

(1). Neither Pilate, nor the Jewish leaders were willing to accept and live with the truth of CHRIST JESUS, and by putting HIM to death, they, at one and the same time, threw their own selves into permanent separation from GOD. We need to be careful not to do the same thing, by leaving CHRIST out of our lives.

(2). Commit today to live in the truth of CHRIST JESUS, and not fall victim to the lures of this world. Take a moment and ask GOD to, in some way, impress upon your heart and mind, the importance of accepting CHRIST'S salvation right now, because tomorrow may be too late.

(3). The religious leaders wanted desperately to find fault in JESUS, and instead, in the end, found themselves desperately seeking to find a right time, so that they could do wrong thing, which was taking JESUS out of their lives permanently.

(4). To not let CHRIST become a part, of your personal life, is always, the wrong thing to do. So, stop looking for reasons why you shouldn't come to CHRIST. Come on over! There is no fault in HIM.

LIFE RESPONSE:

Pray a prayer of thanksgiving praising GOD for CHRIST JESUS, WHO is the TRUTH, and that you will be able to live in, and with that truth, for the remainder of your life.

KEY VERSE: Mark 15:14

DEVOTIONAL PASSAGES: Matthew 26:57-27:26, Luke 22:66-23:25, John 18:12-19:16

# LESSON TWENTY:

## JESUS' CRUCIFIXION
(A synoptic account)

### SCRIPTURES:
The King James Version
(Mark 15:21-37)

(Also referencing Matthew 27:32-50, Luke 23:26-46, & John 19:16-30)

**15** (21) And they compel one Simon a Cyrenian, who passed by, coming out of the country, the father of Alexander and Rufus, to bear HIS cross. (22) And they bring HIM unto the place Golgotha, which is, being interpreted, the place of the skull. (23) And they gave HIM to drink wine mingled with myrrh: but HE received it not. (24) And when they had crucified HIM, they parted HIS garments, casting lots upon them, what every man should take.

(25) And it was the third hour, and they crucified HIM. (26) And the superscription of HIS accusation was written over, "The KING of the Jews". (27) And with HIM they crucify two thieves; the one on HIS right hand, and the other on HIS left. (28) And the scripture was fulfilled, which saith, "And HE was numbered with the transgressors". (29) And they that passed by railed on HIM, wagging their heads, and saying, "Ah, THOU that destroyest the temple, and buildest it in three days, (30) Save THYSELF, and come down from the cross. (31) Likewise also the chief priests mocking said among themselves with the scribes, "HE saved others; HIMSELF HE cannot save. (32) Let CHRIST the KING of Israel descend now from the cross, that we may see and believe. And they that were crucified with HIM reviled HIM. (33) And when the sixth hour was come, there was darkness over the whole land until the ninth hour. (34) And at the ninth hour JESUS cried with a loud voice, saying, "ELOI, ELOI, lama sabathani?" Which is, being interpreted, "MY GOD, MY GOD, why hast THOU forsaken ME?" (35) And some of them that stood by, when they heard it, said, "Behold, HE calleth Elias". (36) And one ran and filled a spunge full of vinegar, and put it on a reed, and gave HIM to drink, saying, "Let alone; let us see whether Elias will come to take HIM down. (37) And JESUS cried with a loud voice, and gave up the GHOST.

**COMMENTARY:**

In Mark 15:21-37, Matthew 27:32-50, Luke 23:26-46, and John 19:16-30, the authors of GOD give their respective accounts of the "Crucifixion of CHRIST JESUS". John and Matthew were eyewitnesses. John Mark wrote of Peter's recollections, who himself was an eyewitness, and Luke's account is, by his own admission, a result of careful investigative work, and interviewing of the early Disciples and other eyewitnesses to JESUS' life and Ministry, here on earth.

What follows, will be my attempt to incorporate these four accounts into one accurate depiction of this tragic and unjust event. All accounts begin with JESUS' death walk to Golgotha (Skull Hill), where HE is ultimately crucified by Roman method. However, Mark, Matthew, and Luke include in their accounts of how, on the way, JESUS and HIS executioners make a divine encounter with a man called Simon, who is compelled by a Roman soldier to carry the cross of JESUS.

Here we see, in Simon, a man who has come all the way from Cyrene on the continent of Africa to, no doubt, participate in the Passover Celebration. Instead, he ends up unexpectedly becoming the first Gentile to perform a Christian mission. And since that fateful moment in time, no man has, or ever will be again, "forced" to carry the cross of our LORD and SAVIOR, JESUS CHRIST. It was, from that moment on, to always and forever be "a voluntary act" brought on by the desires of the human heart. And keep in mind, it was not GOD who forced him, but man.

Great crowds of people followed as JESUS was being lead to HIS death, including many grief stricken women. As they were moving along, suddenly JESUS turned and said to them, "Daughters of Jerusalem, weep not for ME, but for yourselves, and for your children. For, behold, the days are coming, in the which they shall say, blessed are the barren, and the wombs that never bare, and the paps which never gave suck. Then shall they begin to say to the mountains, fall on us; and to the hills, cover us. For if they do these things in a green tree, what shall be done in the dry?"(Luke 23:28-31 - KJV).

In those days, when a criminal was condemned to be crucified, he was taken from the judgment hall, and put in the midst of four Roman soldiers. The horizontal section of the cross was then laid upon the convicted person's shoulders, and he was marched to the place of his crucifixion by the longest possible route. In front of him marched another soldier holding a placard, or "sign" stating what the convicted person's crime was.

In JESUS' case, Pilate had the words, inscribed, "JESUS of Nazareth the KING of the Jews". This was much to the dismay of the Jewish religious leaders, who tried to get him to change it to "HE said, HE was the KING of the Jews". But Pilate probably saw this as his last chance to fire back at the Jewish religious leaders for forcing his hand in the whole ordeal with JESUS' trial. And so, not only did he refuse to change it, but he also had the sign written in three different languages, Aramaic, Latin, and Greek.

In Matthew 26:29, Mark 14:25, and Luke 22:18, JESUS promises HIS Disciples that HE will not drink wine again until HE drinks it new, with them in the Kingdom of GOD. In Psalms 69:21, the Psalmist tells us that JESUS would be offered sour wine to satisfy HIS thirst. We see Scripture being fulfilled in (Matt. 27:34 & 48, Mark 15:23 & 36, Luke 23:36, & John 19:29-30) where JESUS is offered wine on two occasions and refused to drink. These can also be viewed as final attempts by satan to trip JESUS up on HIS promise that HE had made to HIS Disciples, during HIS establishment of the New Covenant at the Last Supper.

We see further fulfillment of Scripture, with the Roman soldiers gambling, or "casting lots" for JESUS' clothing, (Matt. 27:35, Mark 15:24, Luke 23:34b, & John 19:23-24). This fulfills one of the seven Prophesies found in Psalms 22 (22:18), which states, "They part MY garments among them, and cast lots upon MY vesture" (KJV).

There were two criminals, who were crucified with JESUS that day, one on each side of HIM. One, strangely enough, felt like he was in a position to mock JESUS. The other defended JESUS' innocence, and thereby, became the last person directly saved by JESUS, during HIS earthly ministry (Luke 23:39-43).

Standing near the cross that day, were Mary, JESUS' mother, her sister Mary, the wife of Cleophas (who is said to be the same as Alpheus, the father of James and Joseph), Zebedee's wife (the mother of James and John), Mary Magdalene, and the Apostle John. Looking down from the cross, and seeing HIS mother's anguish, JESUS consigns her care into the hands of the Apostle John, the Disciple whom HE loved.

The statement that JESUS made to Mary and John was the third of seven statements, or sayings, that JESUS made from the cross. Here, HE says to Mary "Woman, behold thy son", and to John, "Behold thy mother" (John 19:26-27). The other six statements can be found in the following verses: Matthew 27:46, Luke 23:34, 43 & 46, & John 19:28b & 30a.

At noon, darkness fell across the sky, and lasted until three o'clock. At that time JESUS speaks HIS sixth utterance from the cross, "tetelestai" (tet-el-es-ahee), the Greek word for "it is finished", or "paid in full". HE then bows HIS head and utters HIS seventh and final statement, "FATHER, into THY hands I commend MY Spirit", and HE gave up the GHOST.

There is an ensuing Earthquake, and simultaneously the curtains in the Temple were torn from top to bottom. Later the Jews went to Pilate to request that the bodies of the three be removed before the Sabbath, and that their legs be broken to expedite death. Pilate granted the request and the legs of the two criminals hanging beside JESUS were broken. However, they saw that JESUS' body had already expired and they didn't break HIS legs. One of the soldiers did, however, take a spear and pierce JESUS' body in the side to ensure that HE was dead.

In John 19:34, the Apostle John tells us that blood and water came from JESUS' wound, after HE had been pierced with the spear. We know that normally, the body of a dead person will not bleed. It has been medically suggested by some doctors that JESUS' experiences, physically and emotionally, leading up to HIS death, were so terrible, that HIS heart must have ruptured. When a person's heart ruptures, the blood of the heart mingles with the fluid of the Pericardium which surrounds the heart. In all likelihood, the spear of the soldier pierced the Pericardium, or maybe both, causing the blood and water mixture to spew out.

This passage, by John, is final proof that JESUS was a real man, with a real body, bone of our bone, and flesh of our flesh. The water and blood, which flowed from JESUS' side, were to John, and, should be to all Christians, a sign of the cleansing water of baptism, and of the cleansing blood that is commemorated and experienced in the LORD's Supper.

## PERSONAL APPLICATION:

(1). First of all, I would like for you to cherish this thought in your heart; If JESUS had come down from the cross, it would have meant that there was a limit to GOD's love, for us. But, because HE did not come down, it sends the message loud and clear, that GOD loves us with an everlasting love that has no bounds, limitations, or conditions.

(2). JESUS cared for people, even while suffering on the cross with HIS OWN, extreme stress, and physical pain. This is evidenced in HIS reaction to the pain on HIS mother's face, as HE assigns her to the caring hands of the apostle John, in John 19:26-27, and HIS reaction to the criminal, who was nailed to the cross next to HIM, as HE assures him that, "Today you will be with ME in paradise" (Luke 23:43).

(3). It is easy for us to get so caught up, in our own troubles, that, we don't take the time to care for others right around us. The next time you seem to be going through troubled times, take a look around you and you'll probably find someone suffering more greatly than yourself, and when you do, make an effort to lend them a helping hand.

(4). You can care for others, even if it is in a very small way, even when your own life may not be running as smoothly, as you would like.

LIFE RESPONSE:

Pray and ask the ALMIGHTY GOD for the strength you need to care for others. Stress to HIM how important it is to you, that you become more like JESUS, and for HIM to help you to allow "Self", to wither away, and die from your heart.

KEY VERSE: Mark 15:28

DEVOTIONAL PASSAGES: Matthew 27:32-50, Luke 23:26-46, John 19:16-30

# LESSON TWENTY-ONE:

## THE RESURRECTION OF CHRIST
### (JESUS conquered death and its fears)

**SCRIPTURE:**
**The King James Version**
**(Mark 16:1-8)**

**(Also referencing Matthew 28:1-8, Luke 24:1-12, John 20:1-20)**

**16** **(1)** **And when the Sabbath was past, Mary Magdalene, and Mary the mother of James, and Salome, had brought sweet spices, that they might come and anoint HIM. (2) And very early in the morning the first day of the week, they came unto the sepulcher at the rising of the sun. (3) And they said among themselves, "Who shall roll us away the stone from the door of the sepulcher?" (4) And when they looked, they saw that the stone was rolled away: for it was very great. (5) And entering into the sepulcher, they saw a young man sitting on the right side, clothed in a long white garment; and they were affrighted. (6) And he saith unto them, "Be not affrighted: ye seek JESUS of Nazareth, which was crucified: HE is risen; HE is not here: behold the place where they laid HIM. (7) But go your way, tell HIS disciples and Peter that HE goeth before you into Galilee: there shall ye see HIM, as HE said unto you." (8) And they went out quickly, and fled from the sepulcher; for they trembled and were amazed: neither said they any thing to any man; for they were afraid.**

## COMMENTARY:

The sins of Adam and Eve brought physical death. The Resurrection of CHRIST JESUS brought spiritual life. The Resurrection of CHRIST is the essence of the Christian Faith, and, it is the core of all the Apostle's teachings.

In the Greek, the word used for "resurrection" is "anastasis", and in the spiritual sense, it is "a moral recovery of spiritual truth". In the physical sense, it means, quite literally, "to stand up again".

JESUS' death and resurrection are a symbol of how the giving of HIS life regenerated us, and made it possible for us, to be reconnected into a personal relationship of friendship with GOD the FATHER in Heaven. HE is the bridge that gave us direct access to GOD, for the first time since the days of Adam and Eve, and HE continues to act as that bridge even today.

In Mark 16:1-8, Matthew 28:1-8, Luke 24:1-12, and John 20:1-20, the respective authors of GOD, give their accounts of the Resurrection story of our Lord and Savior, JESUS CHRIST. They collectively tell us that at dawn, on the first day of the week, Mary Magdalene, Salome, Mary, (the mother of James and Joseph), Zebedee's wife (the mother of James and John), and Joanna went to the tomb of JESUS.

They knew where the body of JESUS had been laid, because they had seen Joseph of Arimathea, who's tomb was being used to bury JESUS, and Nicodemus, together, roll the stone over the door of the tomb a day earlier (Matthew 27:61, Luke 23:55, John 19:39-42). The women had returned, on this Sunday after the Sabbath was over, to anoint JESUS' body for burial (Mark 16:1-2).

Matthew records that there was a great earthquake associated with an angel of the LORD, who came down from Heaven and rolled away the stone from the entrance of the Sepulcher. The Roman soldiers, who were guarding the tomb, became so frightened that they fainted.

The angel, who appeared like lightning, was garbed in clothing that was as white as snow. He proceeded to issue a proclamation to the women, that, JESUS had risen as HE had said HE would. He invited them to come into the tomb and see for themselves, and then instructed them to go and tell HIS Disciples the good news, and to meet HIM in Galilee.

As the women were hurrying along to tell the Disciples what had happened, JESUS suddenly appears before them. Upon hearing HIS greeting, the women recognized JESUS and immediately fell at HIS feet and begin to worship HIM. It is all together fitting that these women should be the first to receive the news of the risen LORD, and then, actually see HIM. They had been faithfully there, at the cross, and they had also been there when HE was laid in the tomb. Now, they were receiving their reward, by becoming the first people on earth to experience the joy of the Resurrected CHRIST.

In the Greek, the word used for "greetings", or "hail" is "chairo" (khah-ee-ro), and it means to "be cheerful; be glad and rejoice". In Matthew 28:6-9, we see "the three great imperatives that govern the Christian Faith". First we see the women being urged to "BELIEVE", because in verse 6, we see the angel invites them to "see the empty tomb".

Secondly, they are instructed by the angel to "SHARE" the good news. In verse 7, the angel tells them to "go quickly and tell". And thirdly, in verse 9, the first words, JESUS says to them first is, "All Hail", in the Greek "chairo", which means, "REJOICE".

Any person, who has met and accepted CHRIST JESUS, will be able to live forever in the joy of HIS presence. They will be able to come to rest in the knowledge that nothing can separate them from HIS saving Grace.

No man can give you that kind of religion. For, it is something only GOD can do. Through the Birth, Ministry, Passion, Death, and Resurrection of JESUS CHRIST, GOD is saying to us, that HE loves us, with an everlasting love that can withstand all the suffering that this world has to offer. Amen.

---

## PERSONAL APPLICATION:

(1). Come to know and accept CHRIST and "Believe" in your heart. This is the first step to living a Christian life. We must give JESUS a chance to be heard.

(2). Then you must go out and "Share" the good news of salvation that was given to us, through the Resurrection of CHRIST. Knowledge does not become relevant until it is put into action.

(3). Finally, you must "Rejoice", because you never have to be afraid again. You have security and freedom in CHRIST JESUS. CHRIST frees us from fear, self, other people, and, above all, sin.

## LIFE RESPONSE:

Pray and ask GOD to help you to understand the importance of the Resurrection of CHRIST JESUS. And once you've understood, ask HIM to give you the strength and courage, to go out and share the knowledge of HIS wonderful Gospel with others, with dignity and respect. Ask that HE show you how to tap into the power of the HOLY SPIRIT within, and still too, go before you, to prepare the hearts of those, to whom HE wishes you to speak.

**KEY VERSE: Mark 16:6**

**DEVOTIONAL PASSAGES: Mathew 28:1-8, Luke 24:1-12, John 20:1-20**

## CLOSING REMARKS

"I am the resurrection and the life" is what JESUS said to HIS friend Martha in John 11:25. For JESUS is LORD over both the physical and spiritual life. A person's belief in HIM will infuse in them, a spiritual life that will persist, even after death.

That is why the greatest miracle of JESUS was not raising Lazareth back to the physical life, because Mary and Martha's brother, eventually, would again die. The greatest miracle was, and is, in JESUS' power to grant endless spiritual life, to all, who believe in HIM.

It doesn't take a bible scholar to notice, that, in all of scripture, no one ever died, while JESUS was in their presence. JESUS told Martha, in effect, that those who believe in HIM, even though, they die like every one else, will live again. We are given eternal life, as a gift from GOD, for believing in JESUS, and will never perish. And that, my fellow Christians, is the very essence of the "Christian Hope", and the very core of all the apostle's teachings, and mine.

Larry D. Alexander

# CLOSING PRAYER

Our FATHER in Heaven, the CREATOR and SUSTAINER of all of life, we thank YOU for life more abundant, when we live it through CHRIST JESUS. We are so grateful that YOU had a plan, dear LORD that would allow us, to be re-connected to YOU, in spite, of our sins and disobedience to YOU. We are so undeserving of YOUR great gift of Salvation. We mature Christians now know that for JESUS, the only way back to YOUR glorious presence was through the cross, and so it is, with those of us, who follow HIM. With open eyes, JESUS accepted the circumstances of the cross, so that, whosoever believes in HIM will not perish, but rather, will have, everlasting life. And for that alone we have an eternal reason to thank YOU and praise YOU dear FATHER. And it is in the mighty name of JESUS that I pray. THY will be done. Amen.

And now, may the GOD of peace, WHO raised up again, our LORD and SAVIOR JESUS CHRIST from the dead, equip us with all that we need in order to do HIS wonderful will. May HE, produce in us, only those things that are, pleasing to HIM. For JESUS is the great SHEPHERD of the sheep, WHO, ushered in to us, a brand new covenant, and then HE signed it, in HIS OWN blood. And so it is to the ONLY WISE GOD, our SAVIOR, through JESUS CHRIST, to HIM be, glory and majesty, dominion and power, in the beginning, now, and through all the ages of eternity. Amen.

www.ingramcontent.com/pod-product-compliance
Lightning Source LLC
Chambersburg PA
CBHW081155090426

42736CB00017B/3335

* 9 7 8 0 6 1 5 1 3 5 5 2 6 *